National Curriculum

Key Stage 2 Age 10–11

Letts

Practice Papers

Key Stage 2 National Tests

MATHS

How the Key Stage 2 National Tests will affect your child

- All pupils in Year 6 (age 10–11) will take National Tests in English, Mathematics and Science. These important tests are held in May each year and are designed to be an objective assessment of the work your child will have done during Key Stage 2 of the National Curriculum.
- Pupils will also have their school work assessed by their teachers. These teacher assessments will be set alongside your child's results in the National Tests to give a clear picture of his/her overall achievement.
- In July, the results of your child's tests together with the teacher assessments will be reported to you.
- Results from these tests will be used in the compilation of school 'league tables'.
- It is not the purpose of the tests to aid secondary schools in deciding which children to give places to, but the results may be used to help place your child in the appropriate teaching group.

How this book will help your child

- This book offers plenty of practice in the type of question your child will face in the Key Stage 2 National Test for Maths, including a Mental Arithmetic Test.
- Facts, formulae and an explanation of the core curriculum topics show you what your child needs to know.
- A Glossary of mathematical terms used in this book allows you to help your child understand key concepts.
- The answers and a mark scheme have been provided to allow you to check how your child has done.
- The 'Note to parent' boxes in the Answers section give you advice on how to improve your child's answers and avoid common mistakes.
- A unique Marking grid allows you to record your child's results and estimate the level of the National Curriculum at which your child is working.

First published 1995
Reprinted 1996 (twice), 1997, 1998
Revised 1995, 1997 (twice), 1998, 1999, 2001, 2002

Series editor: Bob McDuell

British Library Cataloguing in Publication Data
A CIP record for this book is available from the British Library

ISBN 1 84315 060 3

Cover design by 2idesign, Cambridge
Cover logo by Starfish Design for Print, London
Project management and typesetting by Cambridge Publishing Management Ltd

Printed in Italy

Letts Educational Ltd
The Chiswick Centre
414 Chiswick High Road
London
W4 5TF
Telephone: 020 8996 3333
Fax: 020 8742 8390
email: mail@lettsed.co.uk
website: www.letts-education.com

Letts Educational Limited is a division of Granada Learning Limited, part of Granada plc.

Contents

What you need to know about the National Tests

What is the purpose of National Tests?

The tests at the end of Key Stage 2, taken by pupils in Year 6, have several functions:

- they provide the government with a snapshot picture of attainment throughout the country, enabling it to make judgements about whether standards are improving nationally.
- they give information to OFSTED about schools' achievements, so that they can judge which schools are improving and which are deemed to be failing their pupils.
- they give you information about your child's progress compared to national standards.

How do the tests work?

In May of Year 6, your child will take tests on the core subjects of English, Mathematics and Science. In Maths there are two written tests and a mental arithmetic test. Your child will have 45 minutes to complete each written test. The tests are not marked in school by a teacher, but posted off to an external marker, who is often a teacher in another school or a retired teacher. External markers have been trained in marking the tests so that all pupils' test papers throughout the country are marked to the same standard.

Once the tests have been marked, the mark is translated into a 'level'. The level that each mark corresponds to is decided according to results gained in pre-tests and the tests themselves. It varies slightly from year to year. The test papers, marks and levels are returned to your child's school in July, then the levels are reported to you and to the secondary school that your child will attend.

What do the tests assess?

The tests are designed to assess your child's knowledge, skills and understanding in the context of the programme of study set out in the National Curriculum. This can be found on the National Curriculum website, www.nc.uk.net. The programme of study is divided into four sections, called Attainment Targets:

- Ma1 – Using and Applying Mathematics
- Ma2 – Number and Algebra
- Ma3 – Shape, Space and Measures
- Ma4 – Handling Data.

The written tests mostly assess Ma2, Ma3 and Ma4, but there are many questions that also test elements of Ma1. Your child's teacher also assesses Ma1.

What are the levels and what do they mean?

There is a set of benchmark standards that measure a pupil's progress through the first three Key Stages of the National Curriculum. Attainment is measured in steps called 'levels', from 1 to 7. The National Curriculum document sets out the knowledge, skills and understanding that pupils should demonstrate at each level. The government target is for pupils to achieve Level 2 at the end of Key Stage 1, Level 4 at the end of Key Stage 2 and Level 5 or 6 at the end of Key Stage 3. The chart below shows these government targets.

How your child should progress

At the end of Key Stage 2, pupils take the tests targeted at Levels 3 to 5. Pupils achieving very high marks within Level 5 can be assessed as Gifted and Talented.

How does this book help my child?

This book gives your child practice in answering the type of question that he/she will face in the actual tests. By practising questions in this way, your child will feel under less pressure and be more relaxed. Being relaxed helps pupils to perform at their best in tests, so we have targeted the questions at Levels 3–5, allowing your child to become familiar with most of the types of question that are asked in the tests.

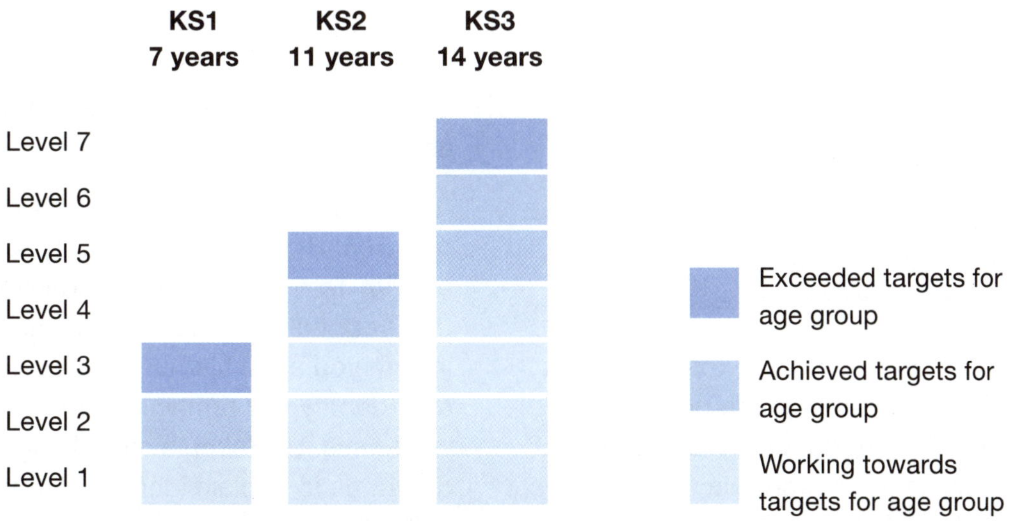

How your child should progress

Preparing and practising for the Maths Test

The questions in this book test the same things as the actual test papers:

- knowledge
- understanding
- handling information
- interpretation and evaluation
- solving problems

What are the key features of this book?

This book contains all you need to prepare your child for the tests:

- National Curriculum requirements – key information for each of the Attainment Targets Ma2, Ma3 and Ma4.
- Questions – two practice test papers targeted at Levels 3–5 and a mental arithmetic paper.
- Answers – showing the responses that will gain credit in the tests and how the marks are allocated.
- 'Note to parent' boxes – advice on how you can improve your child's performance.
- Level charts – what the marks mean in terms of National Curriculum levels.

How should I use this book?

Well in advance of the tests, suggest to your child that some practice might be a good idea. Make sure that he/she is in comfortable surroundings and has all the necessary equipment (pen, pencil, rubber and ruler). Spend some time making sure that your child understands the instructions for completing the test, and then leave your child alone for about 60 minutes to complete Test A. During this time, be available to help read any difficult words or interpret instructions, but do not look over your child's shoulder as this may prevent him/her from concentrating fully.

After your child has completed the test, work through the paper along with the answers and advice at the back of the book. Record your child's marks in the top half of the boxes in the margin. Work out the total marks gained for each question, write them in the grid on page 63 and add them up to arrive at the total mark for the paper. You can then use the charts on page 62 to determine the level of your child's performance on this test.

Before your child attempts Test B, it is a good idea to highlight or make a note of areas where your child did not do well, so that he/she can revise these. Avoid extensive criticism, as this will allow your child to appreciate any suggestions as to how he/she may improve. You could encourage your child to write brief revision notes as a memory aid.

A few weeks later, allow your child to take Test B, using a similar procedure as with Test A. The marks and level that your child achieves this time will inform you as to his/her progress, and identify any remaining areas of weakness. Use simple models and diagrams to explain ideas that your child does not understand and then encourage your child to write down his/her own explanations.

Mental arithmetic is an important part of the National Curriculum and a separate Mental Arithmetic Test is included. The result of this test will contribute towards your child's overall level in Mathematics. In this book, you will be able to estimate your child's level in mental arithmetic separately.

Mental arithmetic questions are divided into three types and are answered within a certain amount of time – 5, 10 or 15 seconds. The different lengths of time correspond to the difficulty of the question and your child should keep to the time stated for each question.

What does the level mean?

The tests in this book give a guide as to the level that your child is likely to achieve in the actual tests. We hope that, through practice, these tests will give your child the confidence to achieve his/her best. By working through the answers with your child, you should be able to improve his/her achievement.

So that you can compare your child's achievement with national standards, the chart below shows the percentage of pupils awarded each level in a typical year.

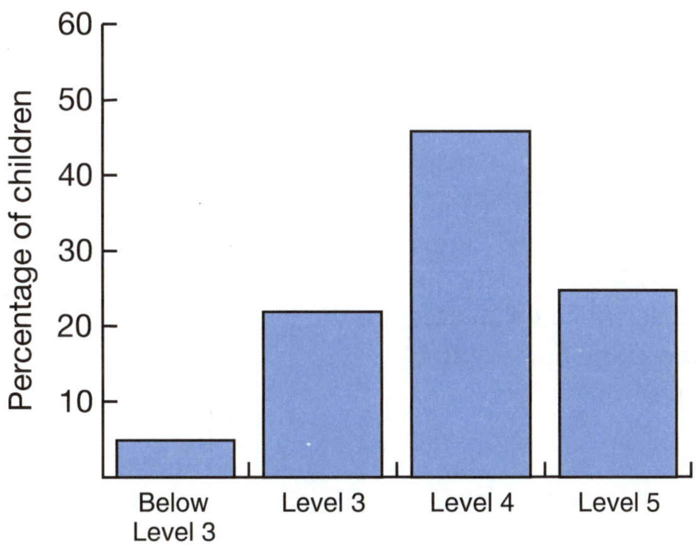

Typical levels in Maths

How do I help my child prepare to take the actual tests?

A few days before the test:

- work through the questions in Tests A and B again, making sure that your child understands the correct answers to each question.
- check that your child knows which test papers he/she will be taking and when these are to be sat.
- double check that your child has the necessary equipment, including a spare pen and pencil.

Finally, avoid putting your child under pressure and reassure him/her about any worries that he/she may have.

Equipment your child will need

The following equipment may be needed for answering these questions:

- a pen, pencil and rubber
- a ruler (a 30 cm plastic ruler is most suitable)
- a calculator. (An inexpensive four-function calculator is all that is required. Do not let your child use a scientific calculator that has too many complicated functions.)
- an angle measurer. (This is probably easier to use than a protractor, particularly for angles greater than 108°.)

- tracing paper. (This is useful for rotational symmetry questions.)

- a pair of compasses. (Use this for drawing circles.)

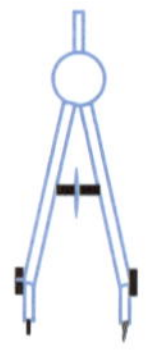

- a mirror. (This is useful for symmetry questions.)

National Curriculum requirements

Ma2 NUMBER AND ALGEBRA

Place value and size of numbers

Your child must be able to order numbers such as 6, 62, 685 and 6453 from smallest to largest and know that the value of the 6 represents 6 units, 6 tens, 6 hundreds and 6 thousands in each of these numbers, respectively.

Your child must know how to write numbers as figures, for example fifty-two thousand and forty-three as 52043.

Number operations

$$\begin{aligned} 2 \times 10 &= 20 \\ 26 \times 10 &= 260 \\ 2800 \div 10 &= 280 \\ 2.4 \times 10 &= 24 \\ 1456 \div 100 &= 14.56 \end{aligned}$$

$$\begin{array}{r} 56 \\ \underline{\times 14} \\ 224 \\ \underline{560} \\ \underline{784} \end{array}$$

$$\begin{aligned} & 256 + 892 \\ &= (200 + 800) + (50 + 90) + (6 + 2) \\ &= 1000 + 140 + 8 \\ &= 1148 \end{aligned}$$

$$7\overline{)395} \quad 56 \text{ R3}$$

Rounding

Your child must know that, for example, 62 to the nearest ten is 60 and 150 to the nearest hundred is 200.

Negative numbers

If the temperature in a room is at 7°C and then falls by 12°C, the new temperature is –5°C.

Decimals

173 cm written in metres is 1.73 m.
102p can be written as £1.02.

$$\begin{aligned} 1.43 + 2.96 &= 1 + 2 + 0.4 + 0.9 + 0.03 + 0.06 \\ &= 3 + 1.3 + 0.09 \\ &= 4.39 \end{aligned}$$

Fractions and percentages

The fraction of the shape that is shaded is $\frac{1}{4}$, 25% or 0.25.

Fractions can be written in different ways (equivalence):
$\frac{1}{4} = \frac{2}{8} = \frac{3}{12}$ ... etc.

$\frac{3}{4}$ of 72 = 18 + 18 + 18 = 54

10% of £168.00 = £16.80
15% of £168.00 = £16.80 + £8.40 = £25.20

Multiples, factors, squares

2, 4, 6, 8, 10 … etc, are all multiples of 2. They are all numbers in the 2 times table. When two numbers are multiplied together to give a third number, they become factors of that number, e.g. $4 \times 3 = 12$, so 3 and 4 are both factors of 12.

A whole number multiplied by itself gives a square number. 9 is a square number (3×3). 3 is the square root of 9 ($\sqrt{9}$).

A prime number only has two factors: 1 and itself. Examples of prime numbers are: 2, 3, 5, 7, 11, 13, 17, etc.

Requirements at each level

Level 1 Count, add and subtract numbers up to 10.
Read and write these numbers.
Recognise and repeat simple patterns.

Level 2 Understand place value and be able to order numbers to 100.
Recognise simple fractions such as a half and a quarter.
Recognise simple sequences including odd and even numbers.

Level 3 Understand place values up to 1000 and make approximations.
Use simple decimal notation and negative numbers.
Recall 2, 5 and 10 times tables and others up to 5×5, and use them in simple multiplication and division.

Level 4 Use place value to multiply and divide numbers by 10 and 100.
Use mental and written methods to solve computations using +, −, × and ÷. Add and subtract decimals to two places.
Check reasonableness of answers.
Use simple fractions and percentages to describe approximate proportions.
Explore number patterns including multiple factor and square.
Use co-ordinates in the first quadrant.

Level 5 Use place value to multiply and divide whole numbers by 10, 100 and 1000.
Order, add and subtract negative numbers.
Use all four operations (+, −, × and ÷) with decimals to two decimal places.
Calculate fractional and percentage amounts.
Multiply or divide, without using a calculator, any three-digit number and any two-digit number.

Gifted and Talented Indicates exceptional performance at Level 5.

Quick questions for Ma2

1 Write out this number using figures: three thousand and six.

306

2 Put these numbers in order from the lowest to the highest.

32 46 23 17 34

17, 23, 32, 34, 46

3 Multiply 27 by 10.

270

4 Find the difference between 1.6 m and 2.4 m.

....

5 Write down all the factors of 12.

2x6,

6 Which of the following numbers are square numbers?

1 3 9 20 25

....

7 What is three quarters of £32?

....

8 Year 6 have 14 boxes of pencils.
Each box holds 12 pencils.
How many pencils are there altogether?

12
× 14
28

28 pencil

9 Work out 264.9 ÷ 100.

....

10 Find the value of m if $3m + 2 = 17$.

....

Ma3 SHAPE, SPACE AND MEASURES

Your child should know that the shapes of common everyday objects have mathematical names.

An orange is a sphere, a dice is a cube, a cereal box may be a cuboid.

He/she should understand the meaning of words to describe 3-D shapes:

long, short, point, round, flat, roll, above, below, thin, fat,
edge, vertex, vertices, face, side, corner

Your child should know the names of common 2-D and 3-D shapes.

2-D shapes

Quadrilaterals

These all have 4 sides and 4 corners (angles).

Square

4 equal sides
4 right angles

Rectangle

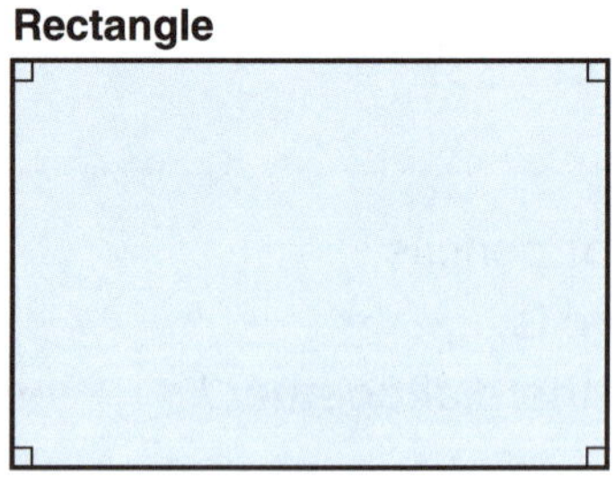

2 pairs of equal sides
4 right angles

Rhombus

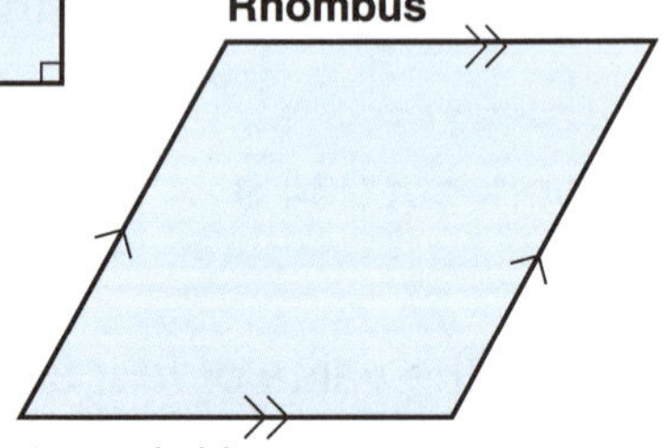

4 equal sides
opposite angles are equal
opposite sides are parallel

Parallelogram

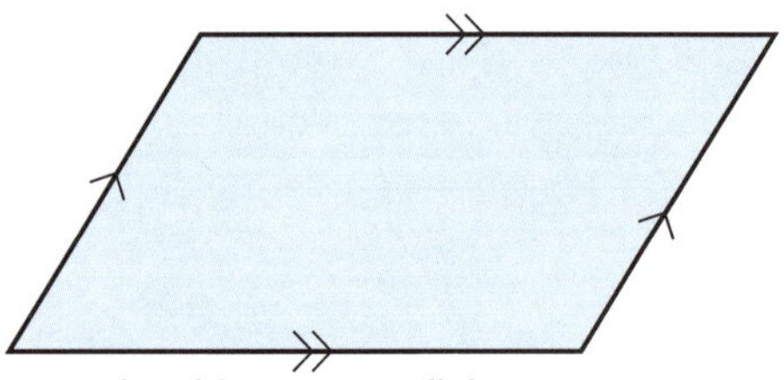

opposite sides are parallel
opposite sides are equal

Trapezium

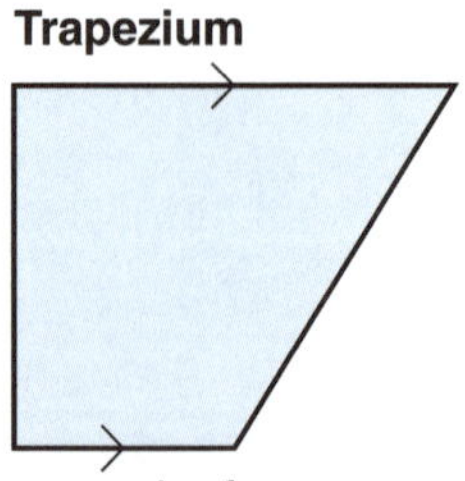

one pair of parallel sides

Kite

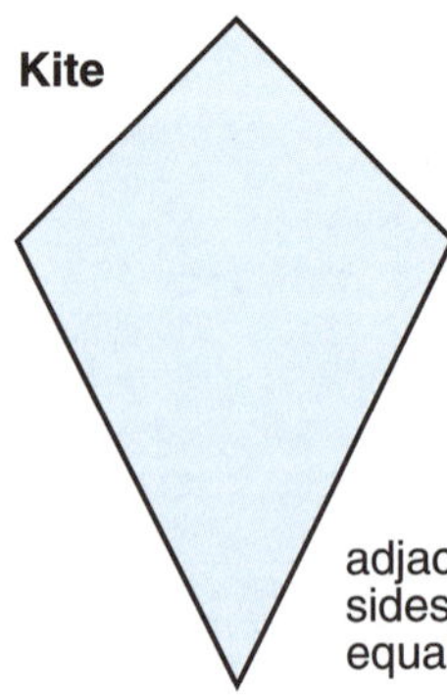

adjacent sides are equal

Triangles

These all have 3 sides and 3 corners (angles).

Equilateral

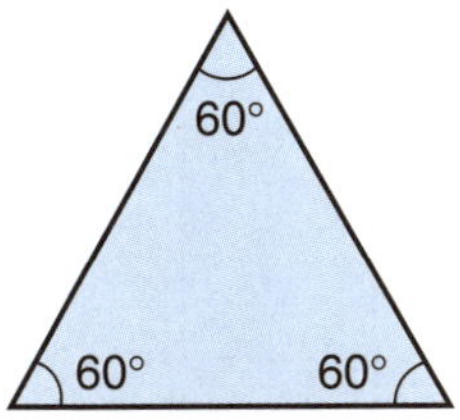

3 equal sides
3 equal angles

Right-angled

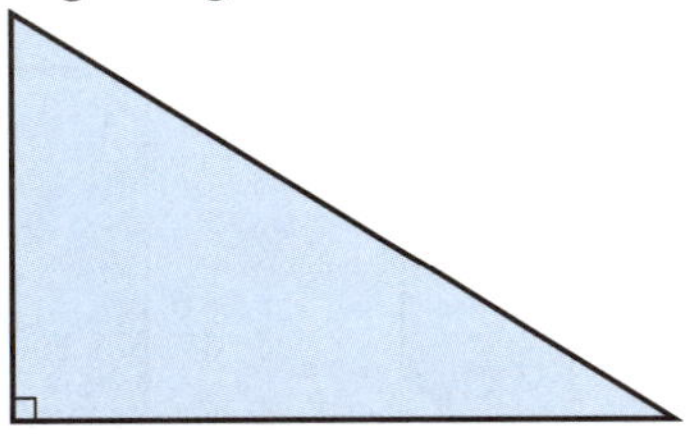

one angle is a right angle

Scalene

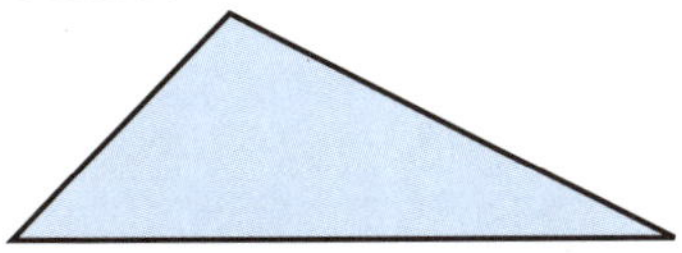

no equal sides
no equal angles

Isosceles

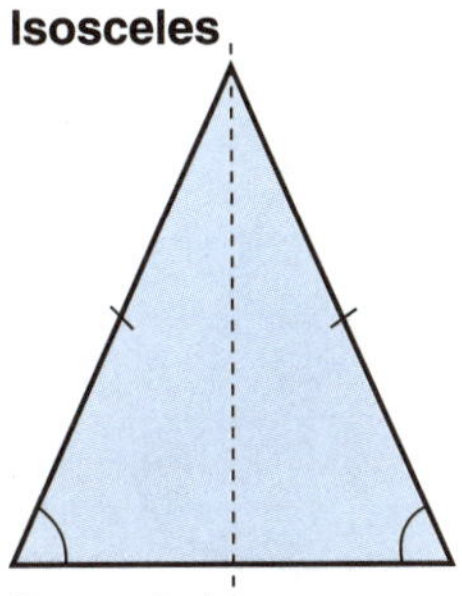

2 equal sides
2 equal angles

Other polygons

Regular polygons have equal sides and equal angles.

Regular pentagon

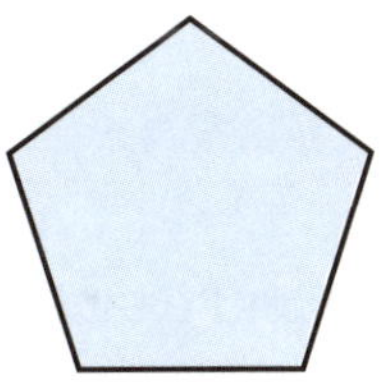

5 equal sides
5 equal angles

Regular hexagon

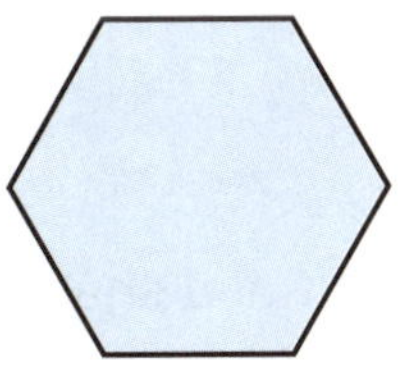

6 equal sides
6 equal angles

Regular heptagon

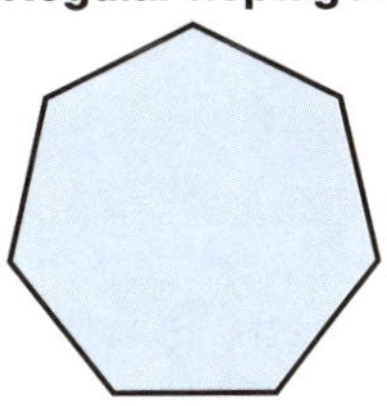

7 equal sides
7 equal angles

Regular octagon

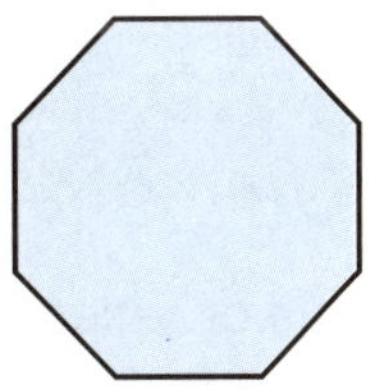

8 equal sides
8 equal angles

Irregular polygons do not have equal sides or equal angles.

Quadrilateral

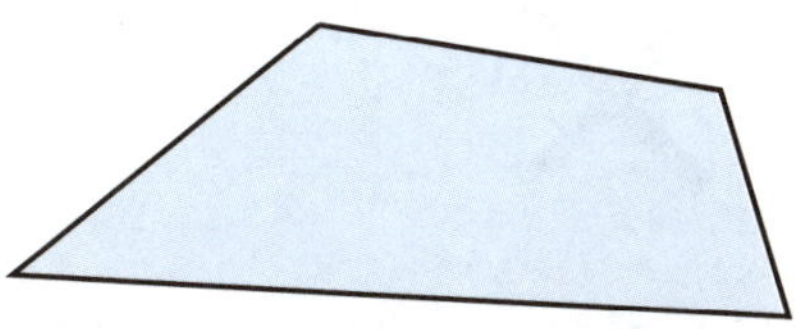

Hexagon

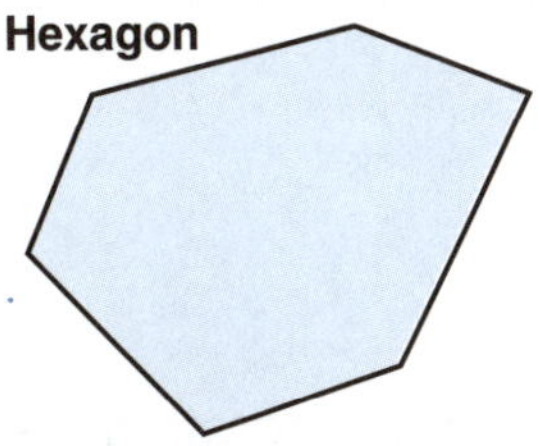

3-D shapes

Solid shapes have faces, edges and vertices (plural of vertex).

Cuboid

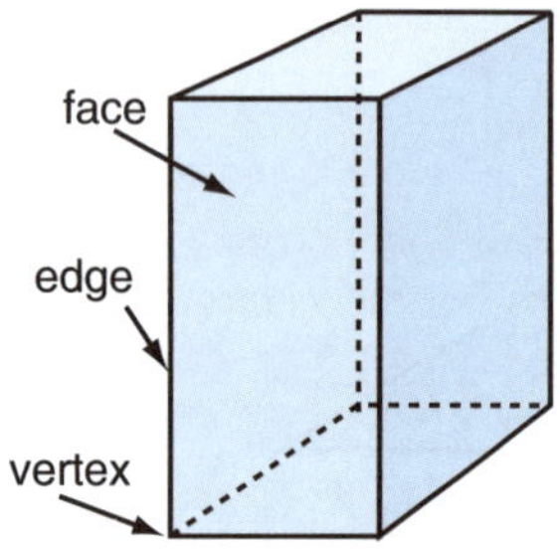

Cube

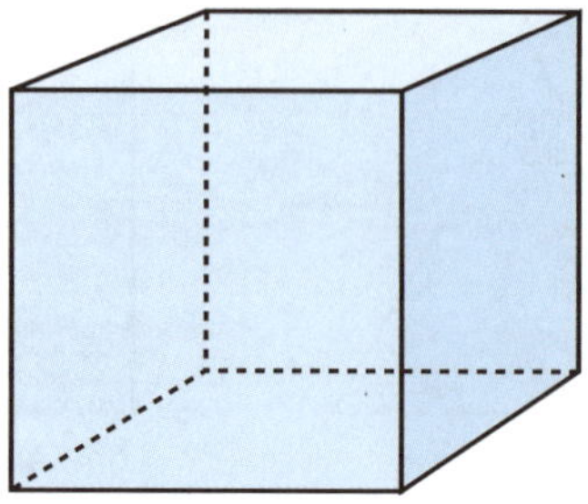

Cylinder

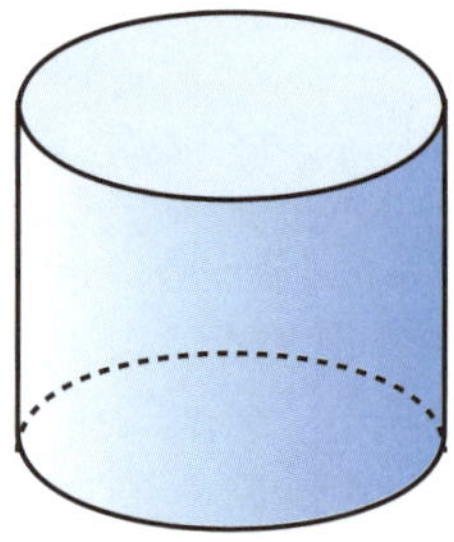

Cone

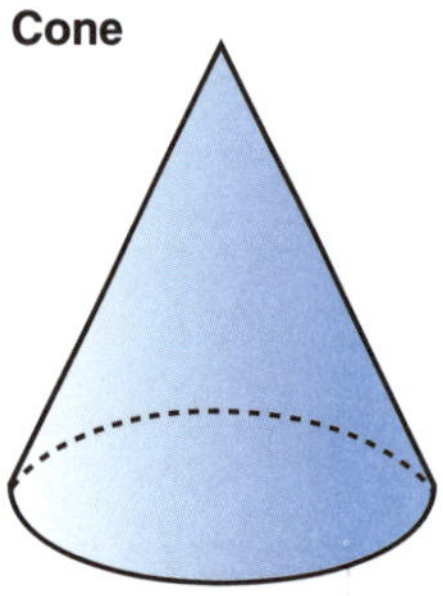

Sphere

Square-based pyramid

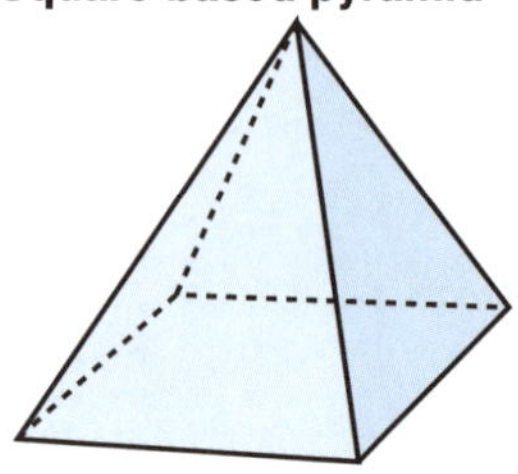

Triangular prism

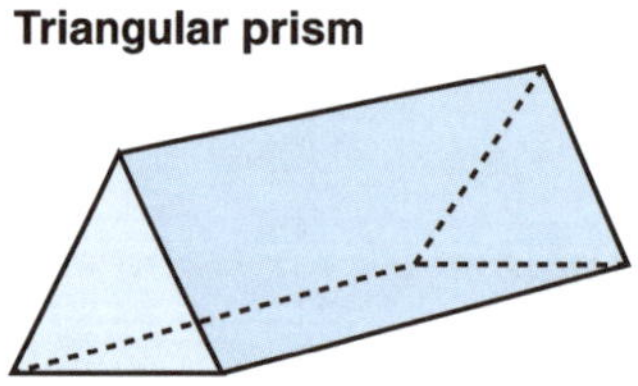

Symmetry

Line or reflective symmetry is where one half of a shape will fold and exactly cover the other half.

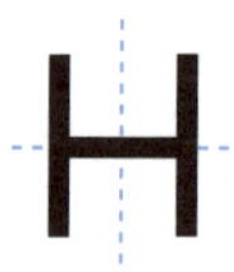

This letter H has 2 lines of symmetry.

Rotational symmetry is where a shape can be turned or rotated and still look the same.

This letter X has a rotational symmetry of order 4 (it looks the same in 4 positions).

Angles

An angle is a measure of turn. Angles are measured in degrees.
There are 360° (degrees) in one revolution.

Major types of angle

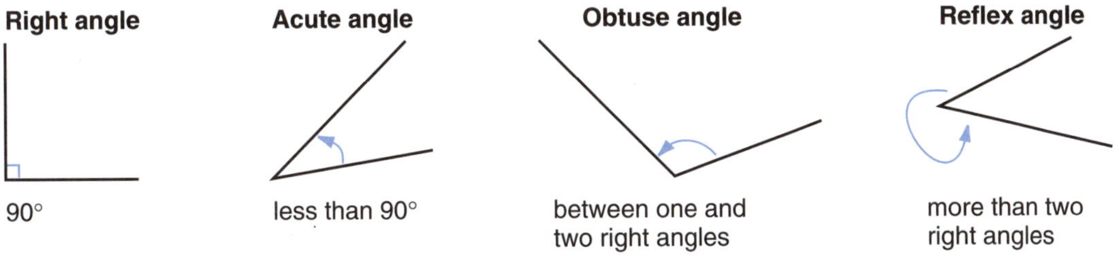

Measures

Your child should be able to:

- measure and compare the length and mass of objects using non-standard units such as hand spans and strides.
- use a 30 cm ruler marked in centimetres and millimetres to measure objects (e.g. pencils).
- use a tape measure to measure the length of a room in metres and centimetres.
- use kitchen scales and balancing scales to weigh objects in grams and kilograms.
- convert metric units (e.g. 100 cm = 1 m, 1000 m = 1 km, 1000 g = 1 kg).
- measure time using seconds, minutes, hours, etc, and calculate the passage of time (e.g. that there is 2 hrs 20 min between 8.30 am and 10.50 am).

Area and perimeter

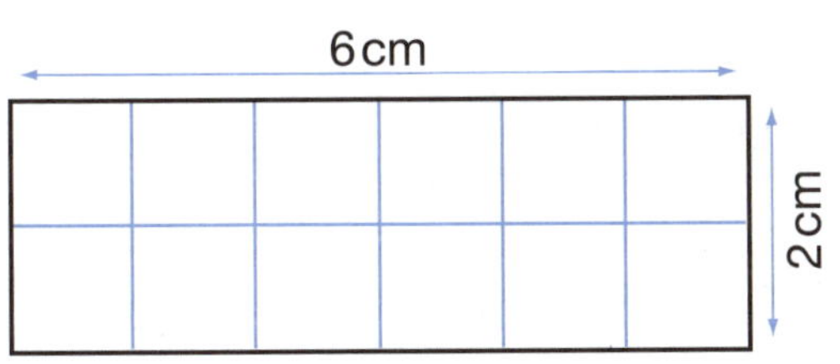

The area of this rectangle is
$6 \times 2 = 12\text{cm}^2$

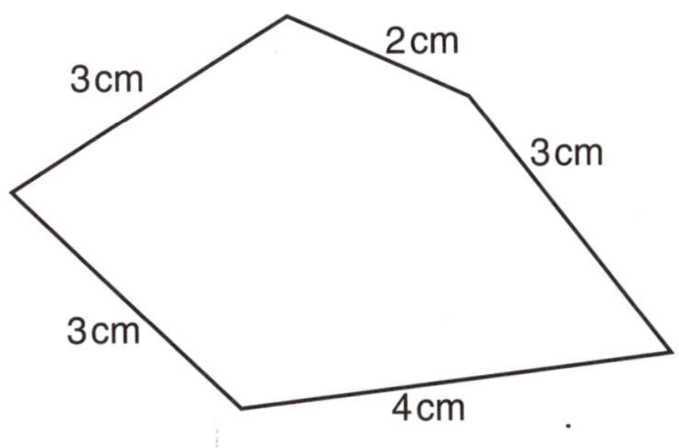

The perimeter of this shape is
2 + 3 + 3 + 3 + 4 = 15 cm

Requirements at each level

Level 1 Describe, using everyday language, the position and properties of simple 2-D and 3-D shapes.
Measure, compare and order objects of different sizes.

Level 2 Describe common 2-D and 3-D shapes using mathematical language and words such as corner and side.
Describe movement in terms of straight and turning properties.
Recognise right angles as turns.
Describe measures of length and mass.
Know standard terms such as cm, m, ml, l, g, kg.
Read the time from analogue and digital 12- and 24-hour clocks, using units of time such as seconds, minutes, hours, days.

Level 3 Classify (group) shapes using mathematical properties such as reflective symmetry.
Describe measures of length, capacity and mass.
Know standard terms such as cm, m, ml, l, g, kg.
Read the time from analogue and digital 12- and 24-hour clocks, using units of time such as seconds, minutes, hours, days.

Level 4 Make 3-D shapes by joining edges or faces and draw 2-D shapes in different ways, identifying shapes that are alike (congruent) and their symmetry properties.
Choose and use appropriate units of measurement and suitable measuring instruments.
Find perimeters, areas and volumes of simple shapes by counting.

Level 5 Measure and draw angles to the nearest degree using terms associated with angle.
Identify symmetries of 2-D shapes.
Know rough metric equivalents of common imperial units and convert one metric unit into another.
Make sensible estimates of a range of measures in everyday situations.

Gifted and Talented Indicates exceptional performance at Level 5.

Quick questions for Ma3

1 Name this shape:

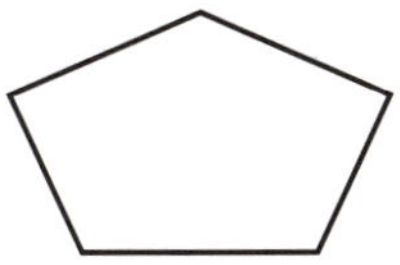

....

2 How many faces are there on a cube? ....

3 What is the perimeter of this rectangle?

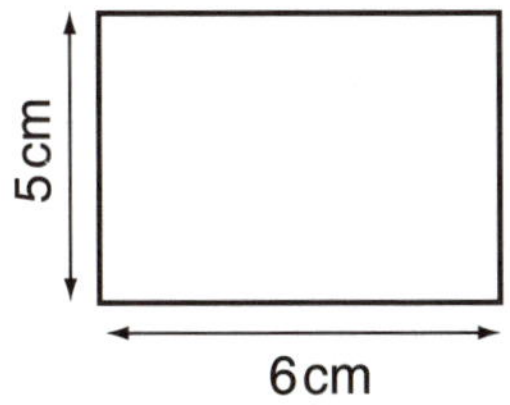

Not drawn to scale

....

4 What type of angle is 132°?
Is it acute, obtuse or reflex? ....

5 Two angles of a triangle are 32° and 86°.
What is the value of the third angle?

....

6 Name a shape that has eight sides. ....

7 How many lines of symmetry has this shape?

....

8 Place the following measurements in order of size (smallest to largest):

2cm 2mm 2.2m 1km 250cm

....

Ma4 HANDLING DATA

Graphs, charts and tables

Figures 1, 2 and 3 below show how the same data can be represented in three different ways. They show the favourite crisp flavours of fifty different children. The results are shown as a frequency table (Fig. 1), bar chart (Fig. 2) and pie chart (Fig. 3).

Figure 1

Frequency table
Favourite crisp flavours

Flavour	Count
Salt & vinegar	20
Plain	10
Cheese & onion	10
Smokey bacon	2
Chicken	8

Figure 2

Bar chart
Favourite crisp flavours

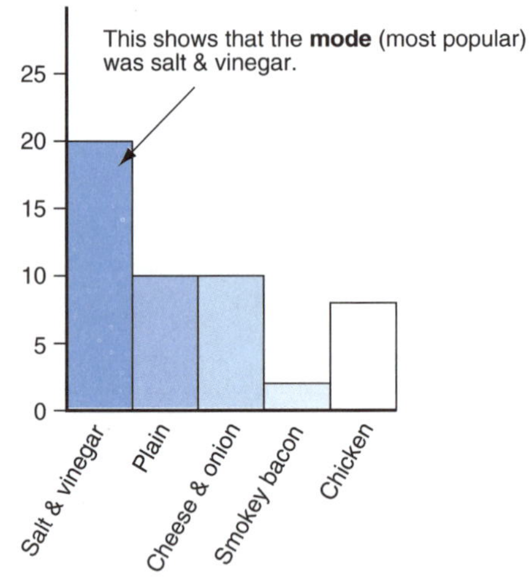

Figure 3

Pie chart
Favourite crisp flavours

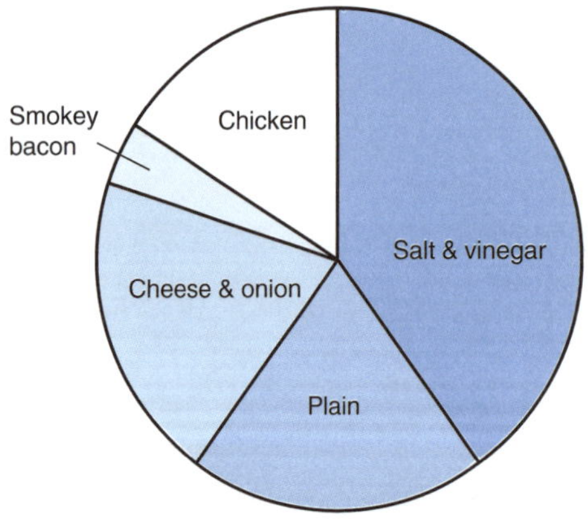

In a pictogram (not shown), each category or object is represented by one or more pictures or symbols. These would then replace the bars on the chart in Fig. 2. Children must be able to construct these tables and charts, and then be able to discuss and use the information displayed.

Averages

The three common measures of average are the **mean**, **median** and **mode**. See Fig. 2 for an illustration of the **mode**.

The **median** is the middle number from a set arranged in size order. For example, the median shoe size of the following: 2, 3, 3, 5, 6, 7, 7 is size 5.

The **mean** is commonly regarded as the 'average' and can be found by adding together all the numbers in a set and dividing this by how many numbers were added together. For example, the mean shoe size from the previous example is $33 \div 7 = 4.7$.

Probability and chance

Events that have a likelihood of happening or not can be shown on a probability scale (line) of zero to one. The zero represents impossible and one means it is a certainty. Most events in the real world lie between these two extremes. For example, the probability of a coin landing head up is $\frac{1}{2}$ or 0.5; the probability of a dice landing on a 4 is $\frac{1}{6}$.

The probability of these events occurring (tossing coins and throwing dice) can be calculated easily, but the likelihood of others can only be estimated after measurements, surveys and experiments (e.g. the chance of rain on a Monday in June).

Requirements at each level

Level 1 Pupils sort objects and classify them, demonstrating the criteria they have used.

Level 2 Pupils sort objects and classify them using more than one criterion. When they have gathered information, pupils record results in simple tables, block graphs and diagrams, in order to communicate their findings.

Level 3 Pupils extract and interpret information presented in simple tables and lists.
They construct bar charts and pictograms, where the symbol represents a group of units, to communicate information they have gathered and interpret information presented to them in these forms.

Level 4 Pupils collect discrete data and record them using a frequency table.
They understand and use the mode and median.
They group data, where appropriate, in equal class intervals, represent collected data in frequency diagrams and interpret such diagrams.
They construct and interpret simple line graphs.
They understand and use simple vocabulary associated with probability, including 'fair', 'certain' and 'likely'.

Level 5 Pupils understand and use the mean of discrete data.
They compare two simple distributions, using the range and one of the measures of average.
They interpret graphs and diagrams, including pie charts, and draw conclusions.
They understand and use the probability scale from 0 to 1.
Pupils find and justify probabilities and approximations to these, by selecting and using methods based on equally likely outcomes and experimental evidence, as appropriate.
They understand that different outcomes may result from repeating an experiment.

Gifted and Talented Indicates exceptional performance at Level 5.

Quick questions for Ma4

Questions 1 to 4 refer to Figure 1 and Figure 2.

Charts showing the number of computer games owned by 5 children

Figure 1

Frequency table
Numbers of games

Name	Number of games
Gemma	4
Kate	6
Frances	2
Joshua	11
Marcus	12

Figure 2

Pie chart
Numbers of games

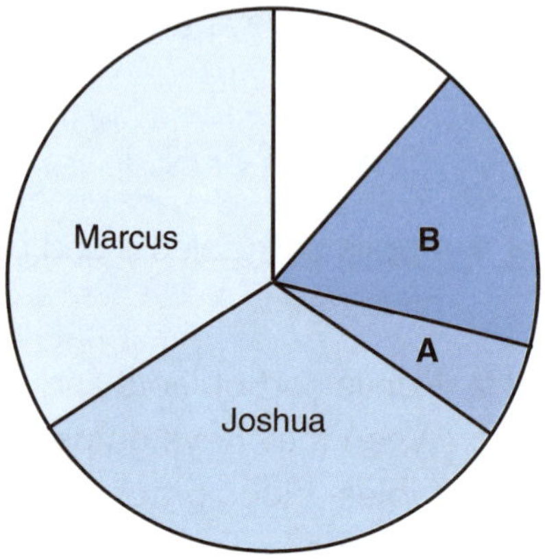

1 How many games were owned by the five children?

....

2 Who owned the fewest games?

....

3 Which children do the segments A and B refer to on the pie chart?

....

4 What is the mean (average) number of games owned by the children?

....

5 What is the probability of throwing a four with a six-sided dice?

....

6 What is the probability of drawing a king from a pack of playing cards?

....

The Maths Tests

INSTRUCTIONS

Tests A and B should each take about 60 minutes. Write your start and finish times in the box at the beginning of the test.

Read all the words carefully. Look at any diagrams or pictures that could help you.

The questions for you to answer are in blue boxes.

For example:

Write down the next two numbers in the pattern.

Look for the 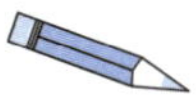 to show you where to write your answer.

Remember to show your working if you are asked to do so.

After finishing a page, turn over to a new page without waiting to be told.

If a question is too hard, you should move on to the next question.

You may not use a calculator in Test A, but you may use a calculator in Test B.

It is best to take the tests at different times (you can even leave a day or two between tests).

A short break after 30 minutes is recommended.

MARKS

Test A

Levels 3–5

Test A Levels 3–5

START	10,35
FINISH	30 mins

2 / 5 Q1

1 The first six balls in the Lotto draw one Saturday night were:

16 27 9 43 38 21

a Put these numbers in order from the smallest to the largest.

✓ 9 16 21 27 38 43

b The smallest number is 9 and the largest number is 43.

(i) What is the sum of the smallest and largest numbers?

✓ 52

(ii) What is the difference between the smallest and largest numbers?

3 4̶3
− 9
34

c Which of the six numbers are even numbers?

✗ 27 16 38

d Which of the six numbers have 3 as a factor?

43 27 21 9

MARKS

2 Chris and John are playing snakes and ladders. John has his counter on 29. He throws the dice and scores five.

a He moves on to number ...34... .

He lands on the bottom of a ladder and moves up to 89.

b He has moved up ...35... places.

1 / 2 Q2

3 Here are four shapes.

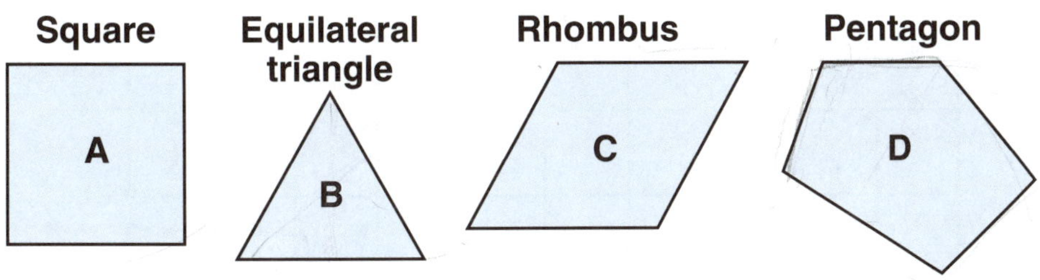

a Finish the arrow diagram below.

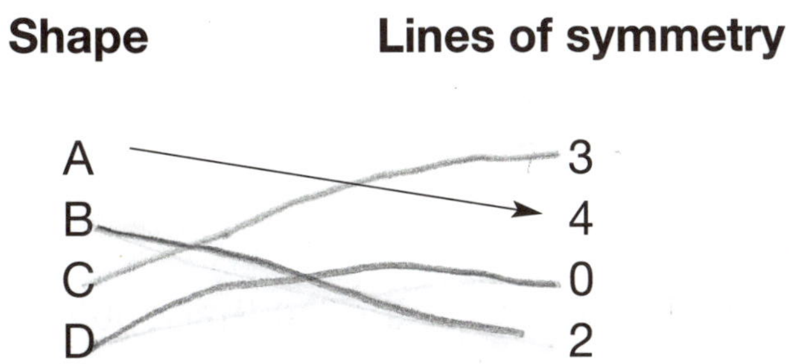

1 / 2 Q3a

b Complete the sentences.

(i) Shape ...D... has equal sides but not equal angles.

0 / 1 Q3(bi)

(ii) Shapes ...A... and ...C... both contain obtuse angles.

1 / 2 Q3(bii)

5 / Max. 12 Qs 1–3 subtotal

4 A shape has three straight sides.
Two sides are 4 cm long and at right angles to each other.

a Draw this shape on the grid below.

1
Q4a

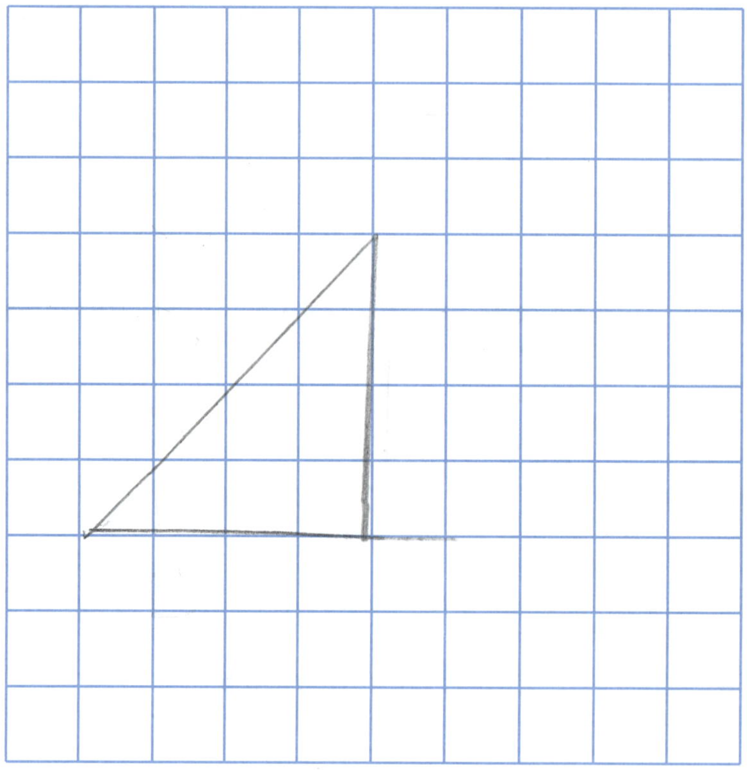

b Put rings around **two** words in the list that could be used to describe your shape.

2
Q4b

parallelogram

equilateral

isosceles

rhombus

triangle

MARKS

5 Here are five numbers:

36.0 **0.36** **3.06** **3060** **0.360**

a Which **two** numbers have the same value?

0.36 and 0.360

2
Q5

b Which number is the same as 0.36 × 100?

0360 36.0

6 Five straight lines meet at a point, making five angles: A, B, C, D and E.

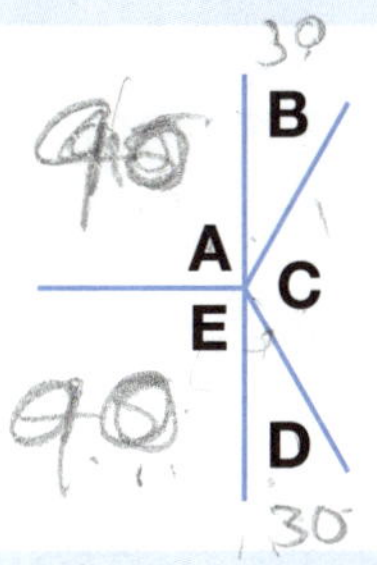

4
Q6

a Which is the largest angle?

C

b Which **three** angles total 180°?

B , C and D

c Use your angle measurer to find the size of angle D.

∠D = 30 °

d Which **two** angles could be put together to make a **reflex** angle? (Tick the correct box.)

A and E ☐ D and C ☑ A and C ☐

Max. 9
Qs 4–6
subtotal

1
3
Q7

7 Owen and Ali are making sponge cakes to sell at a Summer Fayre. The recipe gives the following ingredients to make one sponge cake.

100 g margarine
150 g sugar
100 g self-raising flour
2 eggs

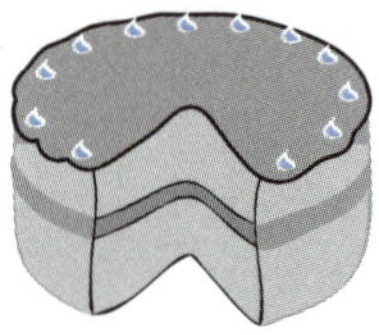

a They have 18 eggs and as much margarine, sugar and self-raising flour as they can use.

(i) How many sponge cakes can they make?

9.

(ii) What weight of sugar will they need to make these cakes?

150 × 9

1350g

b They decide to ice the cakes and weigh out 175 g of icing sugar.
Mark an arrow (↑) on the scale below to show the reading for 175 g.

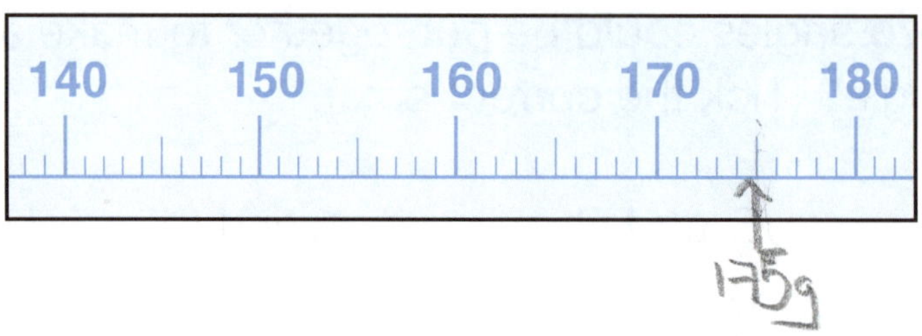

8 Look at the sum below.

Fill in the missing digits to complete the sum.

```
  2 .... 6
+   9 ....
----------
.... 8  3
```

1 / Q8

9 Kate thinks of a number between 1 and 10 for Frances to guess.
She then doubles it …
and adds on 12.
The number is now 30.

What number did Kate first think of?

....

2 / Q9

10 Look at the number sentence below.

Fill in what the missing digits could be:

7 ☐ × **3** = ☐ ☐ ☐

1 / Q10

TAKE A SHORT BREAK.

Max. 7
Qs 7–10
subtotal

1
2
Q11

11 Melanie starts to draw a symmetrical shape on a grid made of squares.

a Draw lines to complete the shape. The finished shape should have rotational symmetry.

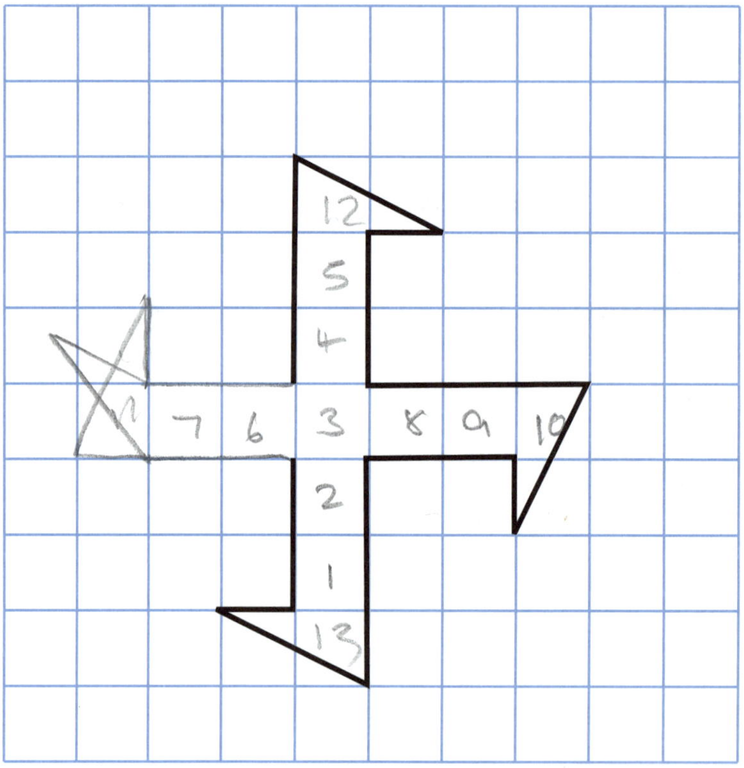

b If the squares are centimetre squares, what is the area of the completed shape?

Area = ...15...... cm^2 X

13.

MARKS

12 You are given this number sentence: **29 × 31 = 899**.
Use this information to find the value of the following:

a 899 ÷ 31 = 29

1 Q12a

b 29 × 3.1 = 89.9

1 Q12b

c 29 × 62 =
(You must show your working.)

198 1798

2 Q12c

13 Rachel and Rashid were using matchsticks to make patterns with triangles.

Number of triangles		Number of matchsticks
1		3
2	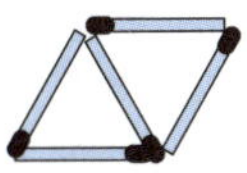	5
3	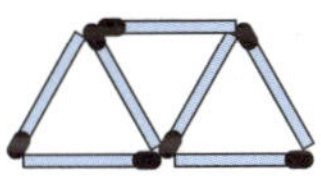	7

a How many matchsticks are shown in the diagrams?

15

1 Q13a

b How many matchsticks would you need to make a block of six triangles? (Do not draw the triangles.)

14 13

1 Q13b

c Explain how you worked this out.

7 × 2 = 14
Adding 2

2 Q13c

Max. 10 Qs 11–13 subtotal

14 Samantha draws an equilateral triangle. Each side is 4 cm long.

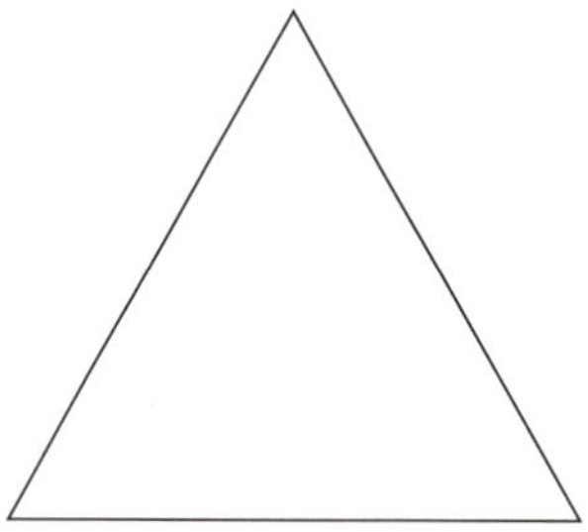

1 Q14a

a What is the perimeter of Samantha's triangle?

Perimeter = ...12.... cm

1 Q14b

b On the grid below, draw a rectangle with the same perimeter as Samantha's triangle.

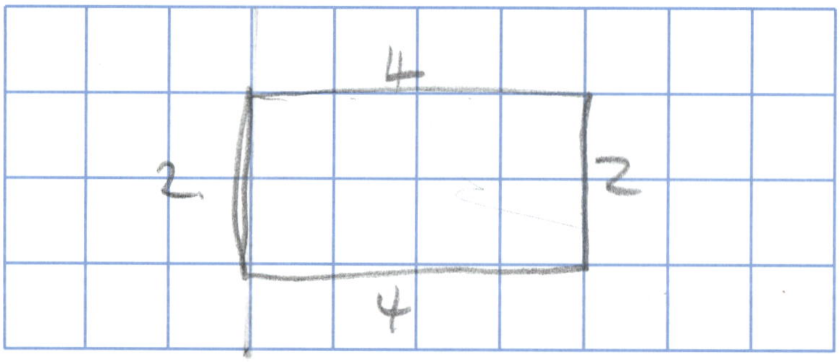

1 Q1(4ci)

c Samantha now draws a square with the same perimeter as the triangle.

(i) How long is each side of the square?

....12.... cm

3 × 4 = 12

1 Q14(cii)

(ii) What is the area of this square?

....9.... cm^2

MARKS

15 The triangle and rectangle are drawn as a graph.
The rectangle has co-ordinates shown at each corner except at the corner A.

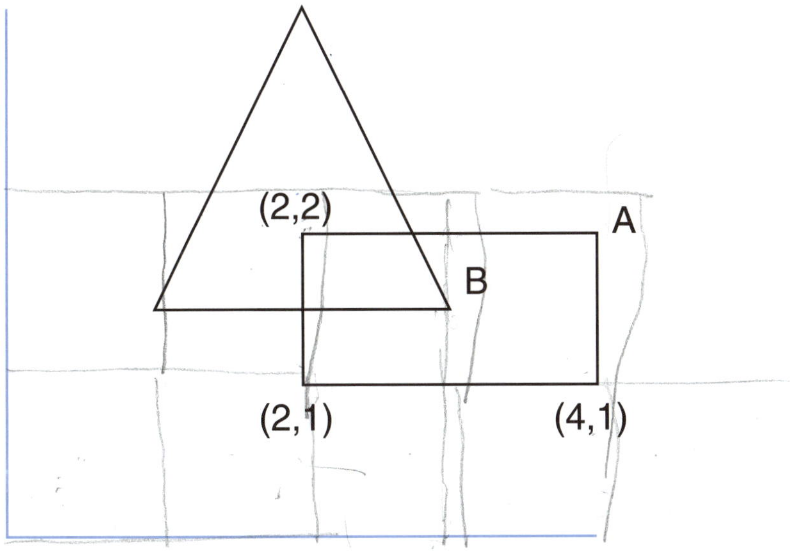

a What are the co-ordinates of A?

(4 , 2)

2
Q15a

b Suggest a pair of co-ordinates that would fit the corner of the triangle at the point B.

(3 , 1·5)

2
Q15b

2
Max. 8
Qs 14–15 subtotal

MARKS

16 'Hurrys' electrical shop is having a sale, with 5% off the price of each item shown.

Radio	CD player	Computer game console
£25	£100	£280

a How much would it cost to buy all three items before the sale starts?

1 Q16a

✏ ....

b How much does the radio cost during the sale?

2 Q16b

✏ ....

c How much would you save if you bought all three items during the sale?

2 Q16c

✏ ....

17 Class 6A are recording weather data. The following table shows the outside temperature on 3 days in January and 3 days in June.

Day	Temperature
Jan 6th	–4°C
Jan 10th	–8°C
Jan 20th	0°C
June 8th	21°C
June 15th	20°C
June 22nd	25°C

-8 0 8 + 25 25

25 - 8 25

a Which day was the coldest day?

Jan 6th × Jan 10th

1 Q17a

b What is the difference in temperatures between the coldest and the hottest days?

20°C × 33

1 Q17b

c What is the mean temperature for all six days?

78°c ×

9°

2 Q17c

0 + 21 = 21 + 20 = 41 + 25 = 66

66 - 8 = 58 - 4 = 54   54 ÷ 6   60

6)54

10

1

Max. 9 Qs 16–17 subtotal

18 Year 6 are visiting the local museum.

25% of the children see the Victorian toys collection.

12.5% of the children buy souvenirs from the shop.

48 children take photographs.

16 children see the Victorian toys collection.

a How many children visit the museum?

1 Q18a

64 children

b How many children buy souvenirs?

1 Q18b

8 children

c What percentage of the Year 6 children take photographs?

1 Q18c

75%

19 Find the values of ***m*** and ***n*** in the following.

a $2m + 3 = 7$

1 Q19a

2

b $3n - 4 = 5$

1 Q19b

3

Max. 5 Qs 18–19 subtotal

Test B
Levels 3–5

MARKS

Test B Levels 3–5

START	3.40pm
FINISH	

1.75
2.75
3.00
4.10
0.40
12.00

2.30
3.20
1.85
4.35
0.80
12.70

1 Ali and Nadir save their pocket money for 5 weeks.

	Week 1	Week 2	Week 3	Week 4	Week 5
Ali	£2.30	£3.20	£1.85	£4.35	£0.80
Nadir	£1.75	£2.75	£3.00	£4.10	£0.40

a After 5 weeks, how much have they saved altogether?

Ali £ 12.70 Nadir £ 12.00

2 Q1a

b If Ali does not save any pocket money during Week 6, how much does Nadir need to save to have more money than him? Show your working.

1 Q1b

c During which week was the most money saved?

Week 4

1 Q1c

2 These steps are made out of odd numbers.
They make a pattern.

Fill in the missing steps.

31	33	35	37		
			39		
			41	43	45

1 Q2

Max. 5 Qs 1–2 subtotal

2 Q3

3 Below is a rectangle puzzle made up of four shapes (A, B, C, D).

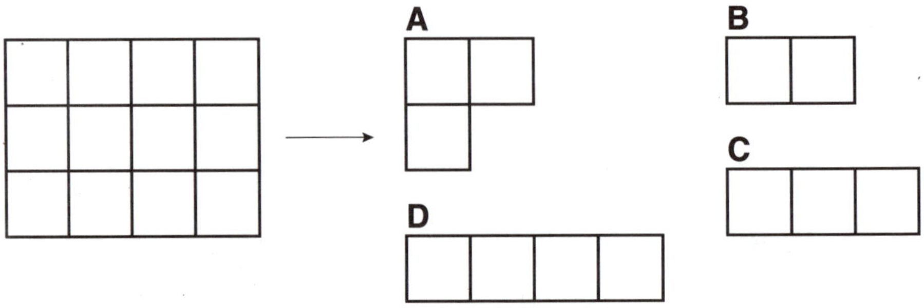

a Which shape is $\frac{1}{3}$ of the rectangle?

Shape A

b Which shape is $\frac{1}{6}$ of the rectangle?

Shape D

2 Q4

4 Two numbers when multiplied together have a product of 192. The same numbers have a difference of 4.

□ × ○ = **192**   □ − ○ = **4**

Find the value of the two numbers.

□ and ○

4 Q5

5 Here is a number pattern: **3, 3, 6, 9**.
Now give **two** different ways to continue the pattern.

3 3 6 9 3 3

3 3 6 9 9 3

MARKS

6 Pupils in Mrs Fraser's class carry out a survey of favourite flavours of ice cream.
The table gives their results.

Flavour	Tally	Count
chocolate	~~IIII~~	5
strawberry	~~IIII~~ III	8
vanilla	~~IIII~~ IIII	9
coffee	III	3
raspberry ripple	IIII	4

a Finish the table.

1 Q6a

b How many people were asked in the survey?

29

1 Q6b

c They showed their results in a bar chart.
Finish the bar chart.

2 Q6c

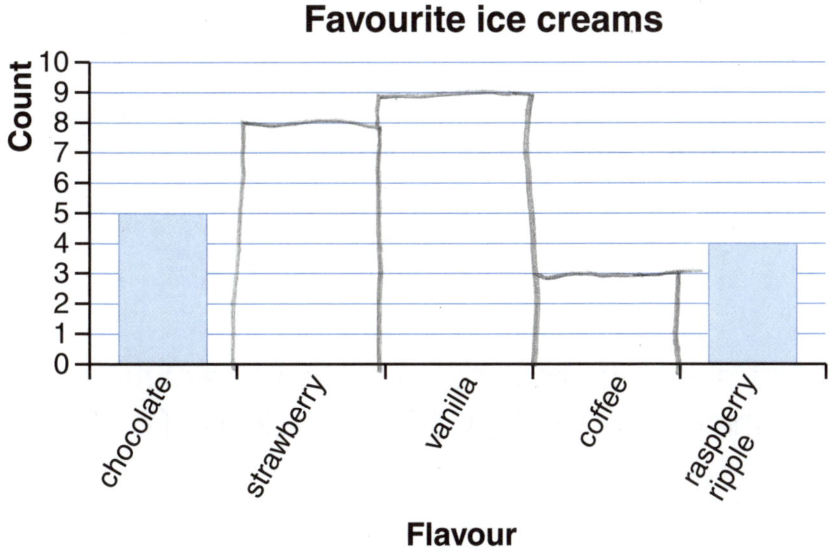

Max. 12
Qs 3–6c
subtotal

2 Q6d

d They showed the results in a pie chart.
Finish labelling the segments of the pie chart.

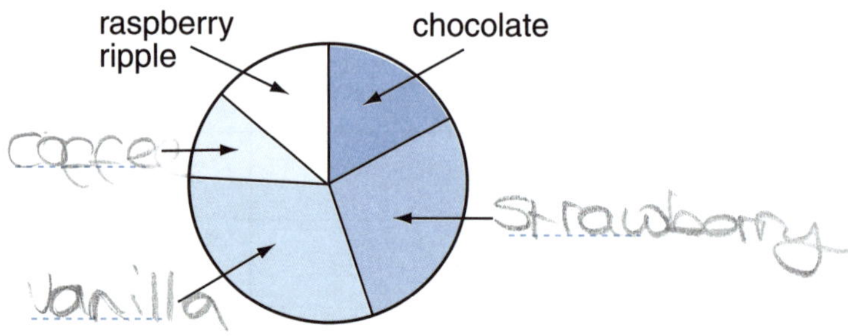

1 Q6e

e Why might an ice-cream company carry out this kind of survey?

To see who likes what ice cream best

7 Gemma and Sam are playing a card game. The cards have decimals and fractions written on them.

0.25	$\frac{3}{4}$	$\frac{2}{10}$	0.01	0.7

1 Q7a

a Arrange the cards in order of size from the smallest to the largest.

....

1 Q7b

b Which **two** cards have a sum of 1?

....

1 Q7c

c What is the difference between the value of the smallest and the largest card? (Answer as a decimal.)

....

8 Below are three measuring cylinders with water.

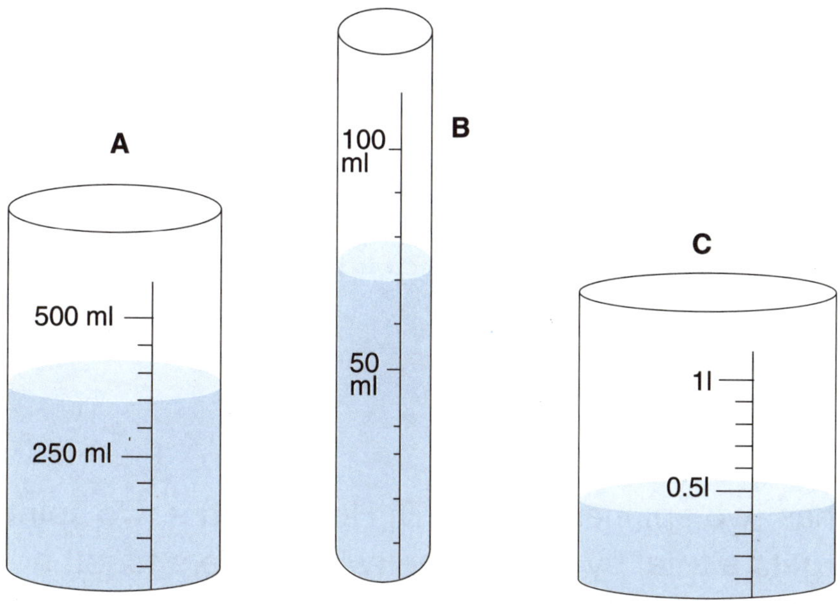

a Write down how much each container holds.

A [350] ml B [70] ml C [0.4] l

3 Q8a

b Which container holds the most liquid?

Container [A]

1 Q8b

9 Andrew enters the digits 1, 4 and 3 into his calculator in different ways. He uses all 3 digits each time.

The first number that he makes is | 4 | 3 | 1 |.

a Write down **two** even numbers that he can make.

| 3 | 1 | 4 | and | 1 | 3 | 4 |

1 Q9a

b What **two** numbers can he make that are multiples of 11?

| | | | and | | | |

2 Q9b

Max. 13 Qs 6d–8 subtotal

2
Q9c

c Andrew then uses a new number key to enter some four digit numbers.

4	5	1	?

Which number key has he used if it is a multiple of 9?

? = ☐

10 Ian has two spinners, A and B. He spins the two spinners and gets a total by adding the two numbers together. Answer the questions on the next page.

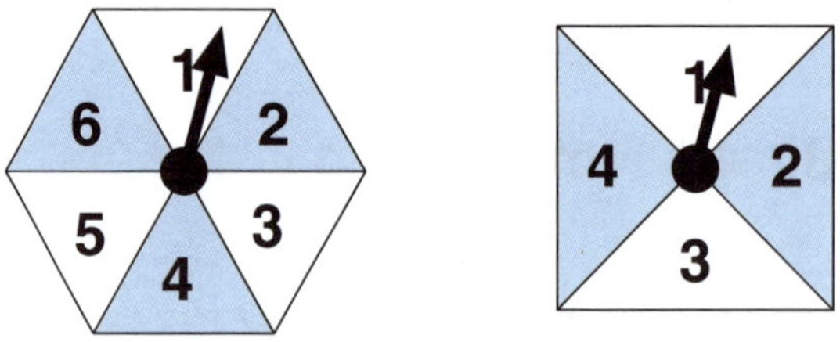

A B

Here is a table showing all of the possible totals. Use the table to help you answer the questions.

Number on spinner A

Number on spinner B	1	2	3	4	5	6
1	2	3	4	5	6	7
2	3	4	5	6	7	8
3	4	5	6	7	8	9
4	5	6	7	8	9	10

1
Q10a

a Explain why the probability of the total being 11 is zero.

Total number will never add to 11

MARKS

b Explain why the probability of scoring 5, 6 or 7 is the same.

~~Bee~~ tottal score will be 5, 6, 7 because 3 you have 2

1 Q10b

c Calculate the probability of scoring 5.

4

1 Q10c

11 Chris looks at the results of seven tests.
Each test was out of 20 marks. His marks were:

20 17 14 11 8 13 15

a What is his **total** mark for the seven tests?

98

1 Q11a

b What is the **median** of these numbers?

2 Q11b

c In which test did Chris score 75%?
Write down this test mark.

1 Q11c

d What is the **mean** mark for all of the seven tests?

2 Q11d

Max. 11
Qs 9c–11 subtotal

2 Q12

12 Look at the number sentence below.
Fill in the boxes with *different* digits to make it true.

(☐ × 3) + 5 = (8 × ☐) + 1

13 These shapes are all made with triangles. The sides of each triangle are 1cm long.

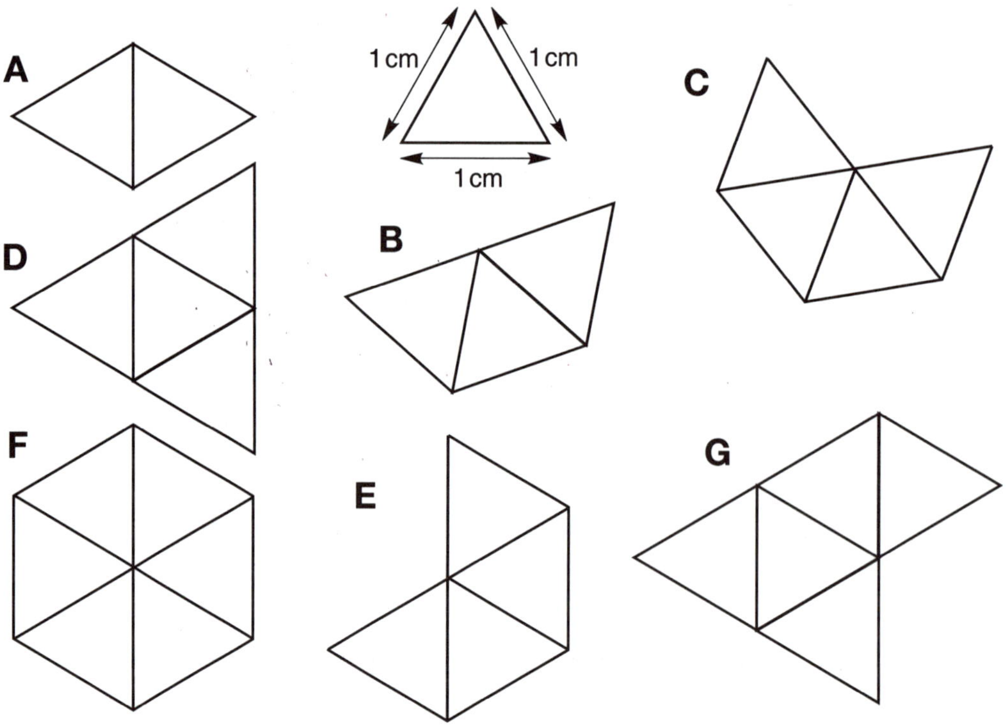

1 Q13a

a Which shape will fold to make a triangular pyramid?

D

1 Q13b

b Which shapes are hexagons?

F, E, C

1 Q13c

c Which shape has a perimeter of 7 cm?

☐

d Which shape has twice the area of shape B?

F

1 Q13d

14 Drawing **A** shows a cardboard gift box. This container can be made from the net shown in drawing B. The flaps are not shown.

A

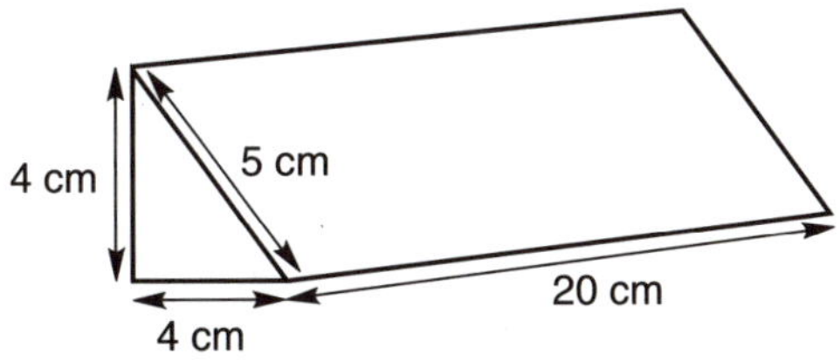

B

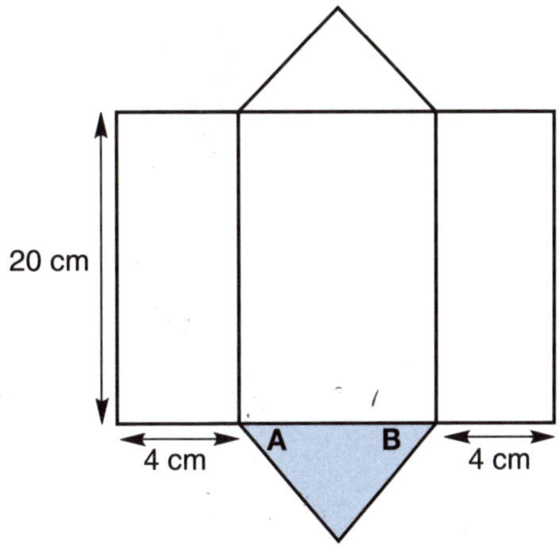

a Finish the accurate drawing of the shaded triangle

A ________________________ B

2 Q14a

b Draw a line to show the height of the shaded triangle. Write down the length of the line.

4 cm

1 Q14b

c Use a protractor or angle measurer to measure the size of angle **A** on your triangle.

....

1 Q14c

Max. 10 Qs 12–14c subtotal

MARKS

15 Mr Patel wants to buy 750 daffodil bulbs. At the garden centre he finds he can buy them in bags of 10 or in bags of 250. Each bag of 10 costs £1.30.

a How many bags of ten would he need to buy?

100 ....

1 Q15a

b What is the cost of 750 bulbs bought in bags of 10? Show your working out.

....

....

2 Q15b

c A bag of 250 bulbs costs £24.
What is the cost of 750 bulbs bought in bags of 250? Show your working out.

....

....

1 Q15c

d How much does Mr Patel save buying bulbs in large bags? Show your working out.

....

2 Q15d

MARKS

16 Sam and Kim are paving an area of their garden.
This area is a rectangle 7 metres by 6 metres.

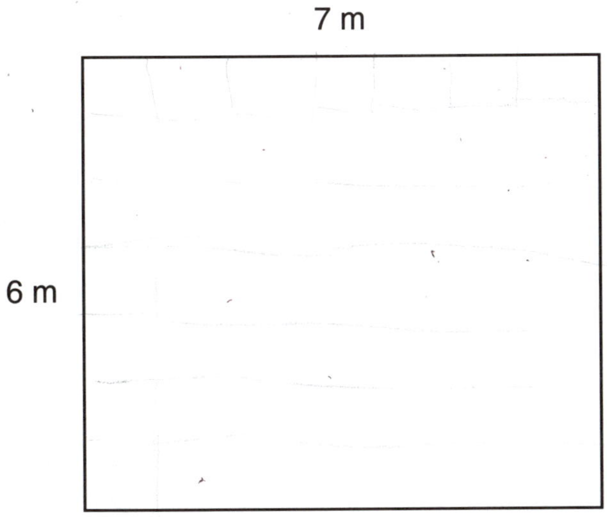

They buy rectangular stones that measure 1 metre by 0.75 metres.

a What is the area of their garden?

42cm²

....

1
Q16a

b What is the smallest number of stones they need to buy to pave this area?

....

2
Q16b

Max. 9
Qs 15–16 subtotal

Mental Arithmetic Test

Ask your parent to detach pages 59–60 and read out to you the questions for this test. You should write the answers on the lines below.

Time: 5 seconds each question

1 ....

2 ....

3 ....

4 .... mm

5 ....

6 ....

7 ....

8 ....

9 ....

Time: 10 seconds each question

10 .... degrees

52°, 38°

11 ....

12 ....

13 ....

13, 7, 4

14 .... Celsius

15 ....

Time: 15 seconds each question

16 ....

17 ....

18 ....

19 ....

20 .... m

Answers

HOW TO MARK THE TESTS

When marking your child's tests, remember that the answers given are sample answers. You must look at your child's answers and judge whether they deserve credit. If they do, then award the mark.

You should pay special attention to spelling. There is no automatic penalty for a word that is misspelt. Look at the word as written and read it aloud. If it sounds correct and has the correct number of syllables, the mark can be awarded.

Above all, as you go through the test with your child, try to be positive. Look for good things that have been done in addition to resolving errors.

Enter your child's marks for each test on the Marking grid on page 63, and then work out his/her level of achievement in these tests using page 62.

QUICK QUESTIONS PAGES 11, 17, 20

Ma2: Number and Algebra

1 3006
2 17, 23, 32, 34, 46
3 270
4 0.8 m
5 1, 2, 3, 4, 6, 12
6 1, 9, 25
7 £24
8 168 pencils
9 2.649
10 $m = 5$

Ma3: Shape, Space and Measures

1 Pentagon
2 6 faces
3 22 cm
4 Obtuse
5 62°
6 Octagon
7 4 lines of symmetry
8 2 mm, 2 cm, 2.2 m, 250 cm, 1 km

Ma4: Handling Data

1 35 games
2 Frances
3 A = Frances, B = Kate
4 7 games
5 $\frac{1}{6}$
6 $\frac{4}{52}$ or $\frac{1}{13}$

Test A: Pages 22–34

1 a 9, 16, 21, 27, 38, 43 — *1 mark*

b (i) 52 — *1 mark*

(ii) 34 — *1 mark*

c 16 and 38 — *1 mark*
Both needed.

d 27, 9, 21 — *1 mark*
All three required.

TOTAL 5 MARKS

Note to parent

It is important that your child can put numbers into the correct order. In part **b**, numbers must be added and subtracted without using a calculator. An even number is exactly divisible by two. If the sum of the digits is divisible by 3, the whole number is divisible by 3 and 3 is a factor. For example, the sum of the digits in 27 is 2 + 7 = 9. 9 is divisible by 3. So 27 is divisible by 3.

2 a 34 — *1 mark*

b 89 − 34 = 55 — *1 mark*

TOTAL 2 MARKS

Note to parent

This question is about handling numbers correctly without the use of a calculator. Your child needs plenty of practice doing this. If your child gave a wrong answer in **a**, but used this correctly in **b**, then he/she should score 1 mark, e.g. **a** 33, **b** 89 − 33 = 56.

3 a **Shape** **Lines of symmetry**

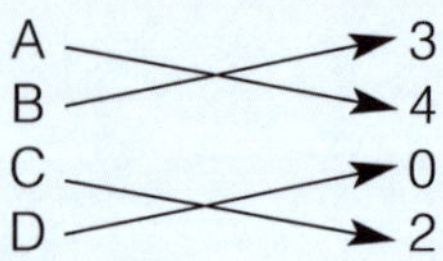

2 marks
All arrows correct for 2 marks.

b (i) C — *1 mark*

(ii) C and D — *2 marks*
1 mark each shape.

TOTAL 5 MARKS

Note to parent

This question concerns shape, line symmetry and angle properties. A mirror will be useful to test for line symmetry.

4 a

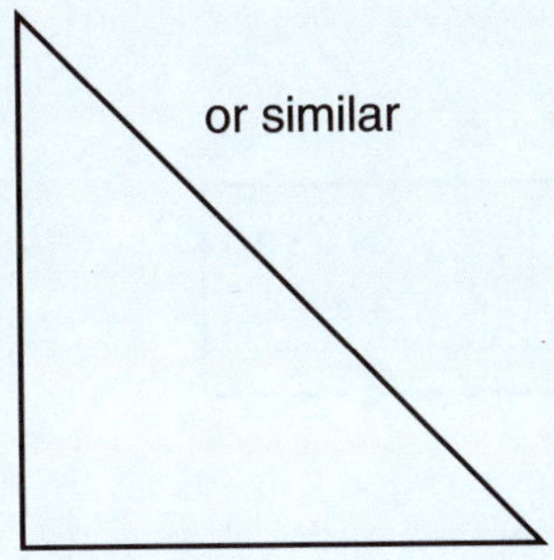

1 mark

b isosceles triangle *2 marks*

Award 1 mark for each correct word.

TOTAL 3 MARKS

Note to parent

Do not attempt to measure the lengths of the sides drawn in **a**.
These are not intended to be accurate drawings but indications of shapes.

5 **(i)** 0.36 and 0.360 *1 mark*
(ii) 36.0 *1 mark*

TOTAL 2 MARKS

Note to parent

This question tests understanding of place value. Part **(i)** involves 'insignificant zeros'. Calculators usually remove these automatically. Your child should understand that when multiplying a number by 100, each digit moves two places to the left.

6 **(i)** C *1 mark*
(ii) B, C and D *1 mark*
(iii) $\angle D = 30°$ *1 mark*
(iv) A and C *1 mark*

TOTAL 4 MARKS

Note to parent

This question involves an understanding of angles, including their measurement, classification (acute, obtuse and reflex) and properties (angles that make a straight line). Accept measurements one degree larger or smaller than 30°.

7 a 9 *1 mark*

b 1350 g *1 mark*

c Arrow marked as shown below.

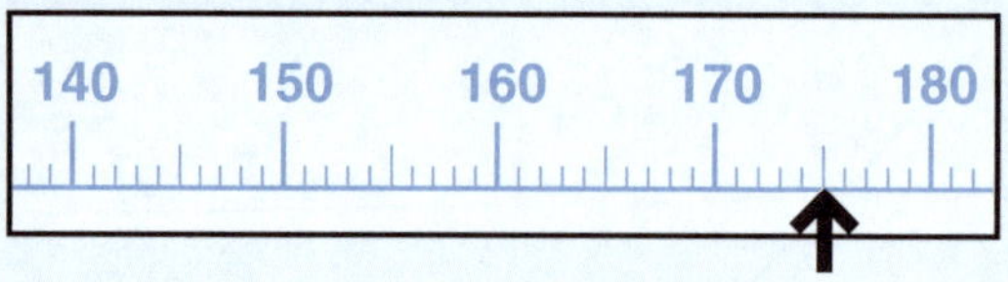

1 mark

TOTAL 3 MARKS

Note to parent

Further practice can be had by looking up recipes in a cookery book and adapting quantities for different numbers of people.

8 286 + 97 = **3**83 *1 mark*

All three digits required for the mark.

TOTAL 1 MARK

Note to parent

Missing digits are a useful means of getting children to think about place value and exchange of hundreds, tens and units, etc. When practising, the results can also be tested using calculators.

9 9 *2 marks*

For 18, award 1 mark.

TOTAL 2 MARKS

Note to parent

'Think of a number' questions are an excellent means of practising mental maths processes and are also a very useful introduction to algebra and the language of equations.

In this question, the statement could be represented as $2n + 12 = 30$, where n is the number Kate first thought of.

10 Various answers possible but all digits needed to gain the mark.
For example, 72 × 3 = 216 *1 mark*

TOTAL 1 MARK

11 a

1 mark

b Area 13 cm^2 — *1 mark*

TOTAL 2 MARKS

Note to parent

Your child may be helped by using tracing paper to trace the incomplete shape before rotating it.

12 a 29 — *1 mark*

b 3.1 — *1 mark*

c 1798 — *2 marks*

Working out (900 + 900) – 2, or similar. 1 mark for answer, and 1 mark for working out but no marks for long multiplication.

TOTAL 4 MARKS

Note to parent

This question tests children's knowledge of number operations and how further information can be deduced from that which is given. In part **c**, no mark should be awarded for long multiplication as this would not follow the instruction given to 'use this information'.

13 a 15 — *1 mark*

b 13 — *1 mark*

c Adding one triangle adds 2 matches. — *1 mark*

Five triangles added, so 10 extra matches needed. — *1 mark*

TOTAL 4 MARKS

Note to parent

This question is about patterns and links with simple algebra. You could try different patterns using matchsticks or counters. Children working at Level 5 and above will understand that the relationship between the number of triangles (n) and the number of matchsticks (m) is represented by $(n \times 2) + 1 = m$. Or $2n + 1 = m$.

14 a Perimeter 12 cm — *1 mark*

b

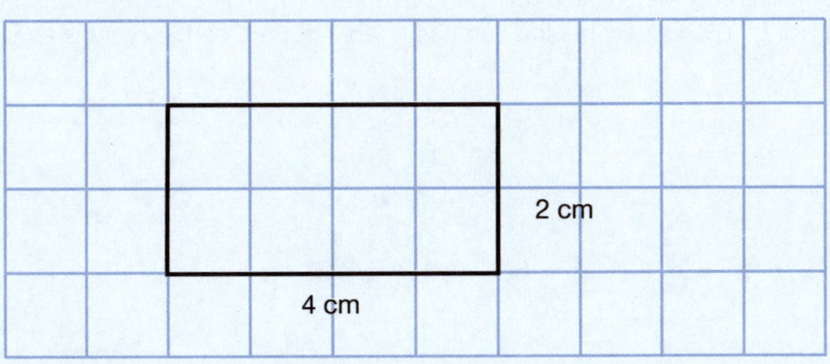

Sample answer

1 mark

c (i) 3cm (Perimeter of square = 3 + 3 + 3 + 3) = 12cm *1 mark*

(ii) $9\,cm^2$ (Area of square = 3 × 3 = $9\,cm^2$) *1 mark*

TOTAL 4 MARKS

Note to parent

Your child needs to understand the meaning of the terms: equilateral triangle, rectangle, square, area and perimeter. The rectangle drawn in **b** may be the same as the one shown but in a different position on the grid.

15 a (4, 2) *2 marks*

Allow 1 mark if one part of the co-ordinate is correct.

b Various answers where the *x* co-ordinate lies between 2 and 4 and the *y* co-ordinate lies between 1 and 2.
A typical answer would be (3, 1.5). *2 marks*

TOTAL 4 MARKS

Note to parent

Part **b** requires your child to recognise that co-ordinates can take fractional values.

16 a £405 *1 mark*

b £23.75
Working out: 10% of £25 = £2.50
5% of £25 = £1.25
£25 − £1.25 = £23.75 *2 marks*

Allow 1 mark for correct working but incorrect answer.

c £1.25 + £5 + £14 = £20.25 *2 marks*

Allow 1 mark for correct working but incorrect answer.

TOTAL 5 MARKS

Note to parent

This question involves knowledge of percentages and how they relate to money. Your child needs to practise working out easy percentage values of money amounts starting with 10%, e.g. 10% of £100 is £10, 10% of £560 = £56, etc. From using 10% values, he/she can easily work out 5% or 15% values as well as many more.

17 a Jan 10th *1 mark*

b 33°C *1 mark*

c 25 + 20 + 21 + 0 + (−8) + (−4) = 66 − 12 = 54°C *1 mark*
54 ÷ 6 = 9°C *1 mark*

TOTAL 4 MARKS

Note to parent

This question involves negative numbers and children need to understand that such numbers lie below zero on the number line.
In part **b** the difference between 25°C and −8°C is obtained by moving from 25 to 0 (moving 25 places) and then from 0 to −8 (8 places) giving 25 + 8 = 33 in total.
In part **c** *one mark* is given for correctly adding all the temperatures and a further mark for dividing the total by six.

18 a 64 children visit the museum. *1 mark*
25% represents 16 children. 100% will therefore give $\frac{100}{25} \times 16 = 64$.
b 8 children buy souvenirs. *1 mark*
12.5% represents $\frac{1}{8}$.
$\frac{1}{8}$ of $64 = 8$
c 75% of children take photographs. *1 mark*
$\frac{48}{64} \times 100 = 75$

TOTAL 3 MARKS

Note to parent

At Level 5* children are expected to know which number represents 100% (see **a**) and to work out percentage values of totals in a range of problems.

19 a $m = 2$ *1 mark*
b $n = 3$ *1 mark*

TOTAL 2 MARKS

Note to parent

There is one mark in each case for the answer. There is no mark for the method of working. Some children might succeed by trial and error. Using 1, then 2 etc., until the equation is satisfied. The better method involves, in **a**, taking 3 away from each side and then dividing by 2 to get the answer.

TEST TOTAL 60 MARKS

Test B: Pages 35–45

1 a Ali £12.50 (NOT 12.5) *1 mark*
Nadir £12.00 (NOT 12.) *1 mark*
b Any amount greater than 50p or £0.50 *1 mark*
c Week 4 *1 mark*

TOTAL 4 MARKS

Note to parent

Your child should use the correct money notation in **a** and not what a calculator displays.
51p is the smallest acceptable answer to **b**. It should not be necessary to add up each week's total – simple quick estimates will show that Week 4 amounts are the largest.

Test B: Answers

2 35, 39, 41, 45

1 mark
All required in correct order for 1 mark.

TOTAL 1 MARK

3 a Shape D — *1 mark*
b Shape B — *1 mark*

TOTAL 2 MARKS

Note to parent

The four shapes A, B, C and D are all fractional parts of the larger rectangle. Children need to know that the whole shape has 12 squares and that each smaller shape can be measured in twelfths. Shape B, with two squares, is $\frac{2}{12}$ or $\frac{1}{6}$ of the large rectangle.

4 □ = 16 — *1 mark*

○ = 12 — *1 mark*

TOTAL 2 MARKS

5 (i) 15, 24 (*1 mark each*) — *2 marks*
(ii) 12, 18 (*1 mark each*) — *2 marks*

TOTAL 4 MARKS

Note to parent

Your child must enter the missing numbers by following a rule. In part **(i)**, the next number is found by adding the previous two together, i.e. 6 + 9 = 15, etc. In part **(ii)** alternative numbers are added together, i.e. 3 + 9 = 12, etc. Other answers would be accepted if it is clear that a rule has been applied.

6 a Strawberry 8, vanilla 9, coffee 3. — *1 mark*
All required.

b 29 — *1 mark*

c Three bars drawn correctly

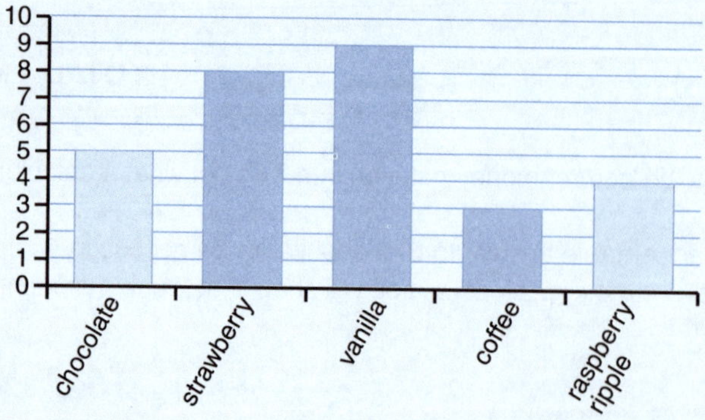

2 marks
Allow 1 mark if two bars are drawn correctly.

d

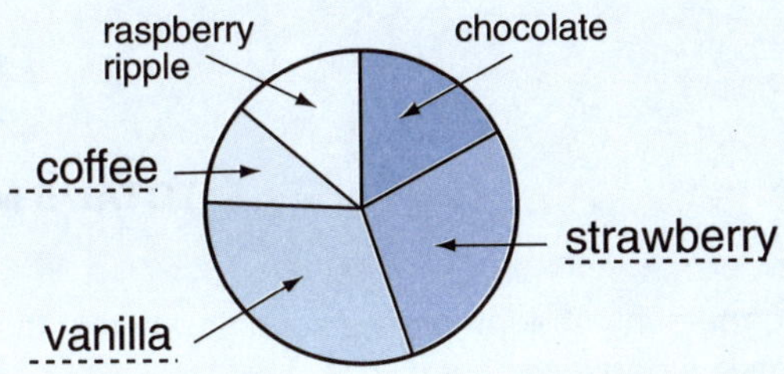

2 marks
All segments correctly labelled.

e To plan the quantities of the different flavoured ice creams that they should make. *1 mark*

TOTAL 7 MARKS

Note to parent

Your child should only be penalised once for a mistake and not over and over again. Supposing he/she gives 9, 9 and 3 as the three answers to **a**. Your child loses the mark in **a**. If he/she then goes on to give 30 in **b** then this mark will be awarded as this is the sum of the five numbers in the table. Similarly your child could score marks in **c** for drawing the correct bar chart from his/her results even if those results are incorrect.

7 a $0.01, \frac{2}{10}, 0.25, 0.7, \frac{3}{4}$ *1 mark*

Correct order needed for 1 mark.

b 0.25 and $\frac{3}{4}$ *1 mark*

c $0.75 - 0.01 = 0.74$ *1 mark*

TOTAL 3 MARKS

Note to parent

This question requires an understanding of both common and decimal fractions and the relation between them. Your child should have a good knowledge of place value and how tenths, hundredths, etc. are represented as decimals. He/she should also know the decimal equivalence of the most commonly used fractions such as one half, one quarter, one tenth, etc.

To find the decimal equivalence of a fraction using a calculator, simply divide the numerator (top figure) by the denominator (bottom figure). This can be done in order to find the size of all of the numbers shown before answering part **a**.

8 a A 350 ml *1 mark*
B 70 ml *1 mark*
C 0.4 l *1 mark*
b Container C *1 mark*

TOTAL 4 MARKS

Note to parent

Part **a** involves reading scales and understanding that divisions on a scale can represent different amounts. Part **b** requires your child to understand that 0.4 l or 400 ml is a greater amount than the other measures.

Test B: Answers

9	**a**	314 and 134	*1 mark*
	b	341 and 143	*2 marks*
	c	8	*2 marks*

TOTAL 5 MARKS

Note to parent

This question requires a knowledge of number properties such as whether they are even, are a multiple of or have a particular factor.

Apart from awareness of even and odd numbers, which are introduced at Level 2, multiples and factors are part of Levels 4 and 5.

A range of strategies can be used to solve parts of the question, but the ability to divide and multiply accurately while at the same time recognising whole number answers on the calculator is important.

10	**a**	It is impossible to get a total greater than 10, i.e. 6 + 4	*1 mark*
	b	There are equal numbers of 5, 6 and 7 in the table.	*1 mark*
	c	$\frac{4}{24} = \frac{1}{6}$	*1 mark*

TOTAL 3 MARKS

Note to parent

Drawing out probability tables is a good way of understanding the topic. Draw out a probability table for two dice and work out the probability of throwing two sixes. Is it easier to throw a total of seven than a total of twelve?

11	**a**	98	*1 mark*
	b	14	*2 marks*
	c	15	*1 mark*
	d	98 ÷ 7 = 14	*2 marks*

TOTAL 6 MARKS

Note to parent

In **b**, the median is obtained by arranging the numbers from smallest to largest and finding the middle one.

12	(4 × 3) + 5 = (8 × 2) + 1	*2 marks*

TOTAL 2 MARKS

Note to parent

An understanding of simple algebra and the use of brackets is needed here. Your child needs to appreciate that the numbers in the brackets should be multiplied before the additions take place. The missing numbers can be found by using a method of 'trial and improvement' until both sides of the number sentence (equation) balance.

13	**a**	Shape D	*1 mark*
	b	Shapes E, F and C	*1 mark*
	c	Shape G	*1 mark*
	d	Shape F	*1 mark*

TOTAL 4 MARKS

Note to parent

This question looks at a number of facets of Ma3: Shape, Space and Measures. It includes reference to folding a flat shape (net) to make a solid and tests knowledge of area and perimeter at a simple level.

14 a Look at your child's drawing. The two sides should both measure 4 cm. A pair of compasses should really be used in order to find the point of intersection. *2 marks*

b The height of a triangle is a vertical line from a corner to the opposite side or base. The height measures 3.1 cm. *1 mark*

c Angle A = 50° degrees. (Allow up to 1 degree error each way.) *1 mark*

TOTAL 4 MARKS

Note to parent

This question requires the construction of an isosceles triangle using a pair of compasses. Part **b** requires a set square or angle measurer and your child needs to use a protractor or angle measurer for part **c**. Try other constructions, e.g. right-angled and equilateral triangles with various side lengths and angles.

15 a 75 *1 mark*

b $75 \times £1.30 = £97.50$ *2 marks*

c $3 \times £24 = £72.00$ *1 mark*

d $£97.50 - £72.00 = £25.50$ *2 marks*

TOTAL 6 MARKS

Note to parent

These questions are designed to get your child to do calculations without the use of a calculator. Parts **a** and **b** involve multiplying and dividing by 10. In **c** and **e** two marks are allocated. In each case your child should be encouraged to show his or her working out in the boxes provided. If your child then makes a mistake with the answer one mark can still be awarded for the method used.

You can give your child further practice here by comparing the prices of products, such as instant coffee, that are sold in different sizes.

16 a $42\ m^2$ *1 mark*

b Area of stone = $1 \times 0.75 = 0.75\ m^2$ *1 mark*

Number of stones = $42 \div 0.75$

= 56 *1 mark*

TOTAL 3 MARKS

Note to parent

This question is testing problem solving (Ma1). There are different ways a child might solve this. The method given is hinted at by part **a** and involves dividing the total area by the area of one stone. Another way involves realising that there can be eight rows of seven paving slabs. Any method that gives the correct answer is acceptable.

In **a**, the unit must be given as well as the number for the mark to be awarded.

TEST TOTAL 60 MARKS

Mental Arithmetic Test Page 46

1	24	**11**	125
2	39	**12**	1110
3	16	**13**	8
4	50 mm	**14**	9° Celsius
5	48	**15**	7
6	501	**16**	£1.64
7	22	**17**	£94.50
8	0.4	**18**	2.10 pm (or 14:10 h)
9	31 or 37	**19**	3
10	90°	**20**	12 m

TEST TOTAL 20 MARKS

Note to parent

You will notice that the questions are of two types.

Type 1 (Questions 1–9) These require recall of a specific piece of knowledge, e.g. tables, prime numbers, simple fractions. They usually require one step.

Type 2 (Questions 10–20) These require knowledge as well as number operations. Questions 16–20 are harder than questions 10–15.

Children working at up to Level 3 should not be expected to score many Type 2 marks.

Mental Arithmetic Test Questions

INSTRUCTIONS

Detach this page from the book. The test consists of 20 questions.

Read out each question in turn.

Your child should write the answers on the appropriate line on page 46.

There are three sections of questions allowing 5-, 10- or 15-second intervals for your child to answer.

You may repeat the question if asked. Tell your child when the time allowed to answer each question has run out.

You should give no further help.

A CALCULATOR MUST NOT BE USED.

Your child should have only a pen or pencil. Working out is allowed, but remember that the time limits make this difficult.

When the test is over, turn to page 58 to mark the test.

Award *1 mark* for each correct answer.

THE QUESTIONS

For the first nine questions, you will be given five seconds to work out and write down each answer.

1 What is six multiplied by four?
2 Add together twenty-four and fifteen.
3 What is two thirds of twenty-four?
4 How many millimetres are there in five centimetres?
5 How many hours are there in two days?
6 Write down the number that is two more than four hundred and ninety-nine.
7 What even number between twenty and thirty has a factor of eleven?
8 Write down two fifths as a decimal.
9 Write down a prime number between thirty and forty.

You will now get ten seconds to work out and answer each question.

10 Two angles of a triangle are written on your sheet. Calculate the third angle.
11 What is twenty-five thousand divided by two hundred?
12 Multiply thirty-seven by thirty.
13 What is the mean average of the three numbers on your sheet?
14 The temperature overnight is minus three degrees Celsius and six degrees at lunchtime. What is the temperature rise?
15 Eggs come in boxes of six. How many boxes of eggs are needed to give forty people one egg each?

You will now get fifteen seconds to work out and answer each question.

16 Hannah buys two folders costing the same price. The coins on your sheet show her change from four pounds. How much does each folder cost?
17 The electricity bill is ninety pounds. Five per cent tax is added to the bill. What is the total bill?
18 A train leaves London at 10.40 am. The journey to Edinburgh takes three and a half hours. What time does the train arrive in Edinburgh?
19 I think of a number between one and nine. I double the number and square it. When I take three away I get thirty-three. What number did I first think of?
20 A square cage for rabbits has an area of nine square metres. What length of fence is needed to make the cage?

Glossary of terms

Area Amount of surface covered, measured in square units.

Co-ordinates Ordered pair of numbers that position a point on a grid, e.g. (5,6).

Difference An amount that separates two numbers, e.g. the difference between 9 and 20 is 11.

Even number A whole number exactly divisible by two.

Factor A whole number that divides exactly into a second number, e.g. 4 is a factor of 12.

Hexagons A plane (2-D) shape with six sides. A regular hexagon has six equal sides and angles.

Mean/average A sum of numbers divided by the number of numbers counted, e.g. the mean of 3, 5, 7 and 9 is $(3 + 5 + 7 + 9) \div 4 = 6$.

Median Another measure of average where the numbers in a set are arranged in ascending order. The median is the middle number. If there are two middle numbers, the median is the mean of these two numbers.

Mode Another measure of average, the most common number in a set.

Multiples Multiples are found by multiplying by a specific number, e.g. multiples of 3 are 3, 6, 9, 12, 15, etc., which are all in the three times table.

Odd numbers Whole numbers that are not exactly divisible by two (leaving a remainder).

Parallelogram A four-sided shape in which opposite sides are parallel.

Perimeter Distance or length all the way round the boundary of a plane shape.

Pie chart A circular diagram used to represent data in which the parts or segments show different categories.

Product A number obtained when two or more numbers are multiplied together, e.g. the product of 4 and 7 is 28.

Pyramid A solid (3-D) shape that has triangular faces leaving a base to meet at a point.

Quadrilateral A four-sided plane shape, e.g. square, rectangle and rhombus.

Rectangle A four-sided shape in which opposite sides are equal and all angles are right angles.

Rhombus A parallelogram with all sides equal.

Sum The result of adding together two or more numbers, e.g. the sum of 3, 6 and 9 is $3 + 6 + 9 = 18$.

Symmetry:

- **reflective** Where one half of a plane shape corresponds exactly to the other half. Also known as **mirror symmetry**.
- **rotational** A shape has rotational symmetry if, when turned, it still fits its outline exactly.

Triangle:

- **equilateral** A three-sided shape where all sides and angles are equal.
- **isosceles** A three-sided shape where two sides and two angles are equal.

Determining your child's level

FINDING YOUR CHILD'S LEVEL IN TESTS A AND B

When you have marked a test, enter the total number of marks your child scored for each question on the Marking grid overleaf. Then add them up and enter the test total on the grid.

Using the total for each test, look at the chart below to determine your child's level for each test.

Test A or Test B

Level 2 or below	Level 3	Level 4	Level 5	Gifted & Talented
up to 15	16–26	27–39	40–51	52+

FINDING YOUR CHILD'S OVERALL LEVEL IN MATHEMATICS

After you have worked out separate levels for Tests A and B, add up your child's total marks for the two tests. Use this total and the chart below to determine your child's overall level in Mathematics. The chart also shows you how your child's level in these tests compares with the target level for his/her age group.

Total for Tests A and B

Level 2 or below	Level 3	Level 4	Level 5	Gifted & Talented
up to 31	32–53	54–79	80–102	103+
Working towards target level for age group		Working at target level	Working beyond target level	Exceptional performance

FINDING YOUR CHILD'S LEVEL IN THE MENTAL ARITHMETIC TEST

The table below will enable you to estimate your child's level for mental arithmetic.

Level 3	Level 4	Level 5	Gifted & Talented
up to 6	7–10	11–17	18+

In the National Test, your child's performance in the Mental Arithmetic Test will contribute to his/her overall level in Mathematics.

Marking grid

Test A Pages 22–34

Question	Marks available	Marks scored	Question	Marks available	Marks scored
1	5	2	11	2	1
2	2	1	12	4	1
3	5	2	13	4	1
4	3	3	14	4	1
5	2	0	15	4	0
6	4	2	16	5	1
7	3	1	17	4	0
8	1	0	18	3	0
9	2	0	19	2	0
10	1	0	**Total**	**60**	16.

Test B Pages 35–45

Question	Marks available	Marks scored	Question	Marks available	Marks scored
1	4		9	5	
2	1		10	3	
3	2		11	6	
4	2		12	2	
5	4		13	4	
6	7		14	4	
7	3		15	6	
8	4		16	3	
			Total	**60**	

Mental Arithmetic Test Page 46

Marks available	Marks scored
20	

Also available from Letts

More essential reading from the brand leaders in home study

Achieve SATs success with our Key Stage 2 Success Guides available in Maths, English and Science.

Brightly coloured and easy to use revision guides

RRP: £3.99

Practise those exam questions with Key Stage 2 Questions & Answers also available in Maths, English and Science.

Practice Questions & Answers

RRP: £2.99

Available at all good bookshops, or visit www.letts-education.com

To register and receive your free book simply log on to:

www.letts-education.com†

or send your details‡ (Name, Age, School year, Address, Postcode, Email) to:
Free Book Offer, Letts Educational,
414 Chiswick High Road, London W4 5TF

† For e-mail registration: postage and packing payable as detailed on the website.

‡ For postal registrations: in order to receive your free book, please send a self addressed envelope with stamps to the value of £1.

Letts Educational reserve the right to close this promotion without prior notification. No purchase necessary.

FREE BOOK
worth £3.50 or more when you register on our website today

GAZZA!

Interviews by: **John Fennelly**

Photos by: Bob Thomas and Monte Fresco
Action Images
Allsport

Designed by: JT Design Consultants Ltd

Edited by: Ruth Bickersteth

Printed by: Edwin Snell

CONTENTS

Page

COCKEREL BOOKS LTD

Introduction

Well, looking back over my first season with Tottenham Hotspur I can certainly say I've enjoyed myself. Although as a team we didn't win anything, we finished the season strongly - which just makes us all believe we will achieve much more this season.

1989-90 is going to be great with Spurs, and as I write this I'm recovering from an ankle operation, which should ensure I'll be available for all the fixtures. I was disappointed to miss out on a few last season, but hopefully by the time you read this I'll have been in action in a good few matches - so watch out everyone!

Anyway, I hope you enjoy this book - and don't forget to enter the competition on page 49 Good luck!

Paul Gascoigne

Paul Gascoigne
June 1989

Gazzas SEASON 1988–89

The postponement of Tottenham's first fixture of last season against Coventry City at White Hart Lane, meant Paul Gascoigne started the campaign on familiar territory back in September.

His Spurs debut was against his old club, Newcastle United, at St James's Park and it certainly gave the media something to write about. Gazza had to endure continual barracking from the Newcastle faithful as he helped Spurs to a 2-2 draw.

The visit of north London rivals, Arsenal, brought Gazza's long-awaited home debut. He scored his first goal in his new colours - with a stockinged foot, having lost his boot - but it was not enough as the Gunners ran out 3-2 victors.

A 1-1 draw at Anfield was next, and then victory at home to newly promoted Middlesbrough. A 1-1 draw with Notts County at Meadow Lane was followed by two 2-2 deadlocks with Manchester United and Charlton Athletic, before Gazza's curling free-kick (the first of several specialist kicks during the season) helped Spurs beat Notts County at White Hart Lane and saw them through to the next round of the Littlewoods Cup.

Disappointing defeats at Norwich (1-3), at home to Southampton (1-2) and at Aston Villa (1-2) were followed by a goalless Littlewoods encounter at home to Blackburn Rovers. A 1-3 defeat at the hands of Derby County preceded the 2-1 replay victory at Blackburn.

Gazza had a hand in Guy Butters' debut goal as Tottenham defeated Wimbledon 3-2 at home, and then was in irrepressible form in the 1-1 draw with Coventry City at White Hart Lane.

The Queens Park Rangers 'keeper, David Seaman, became the latest victim of a Paul Gascoigne free-kick in a 2-2 draw at The Lane, but defeat at Southampton knocked Spurs out of the Littlewoods Cup 1-2 and was followed by a 0-1 loss at Everton.

Thrills and skills by Gazza with the visit of Millwall had the Sunday papers singing his praises as he curled yet another free-kick home from the edge of the box.

Forty-five minutes of sheer quality had the Upton Park crowd mesmerised by his tricks, but an ankle injury forced him to retire at half-time as Spurs ran out 2-0 winners. He then missed the next three matches.

Goalless with Luton Town and victory over visiting Newcastle United by 2-0 saw out the old year at White Hart Lane, but the scores were reversed at Highbury in the televised clash with Arsenal. Disappointment too in the FA

Cup as Tottenham went crashing at Bradford City 0-1.

Gazza returned to action as a 60th minute substitute in the 1-2 televised defeat by Nottingham Forest and then started the game at Middlesbrough as his side were held to a 2-2 draw.

A slender 0-1 defeat at Old Trafford and a draw with Charlton Athletic at White Hart Lane followed before Spurs returned to winning ways.

Gazza's 13th minute strike helped them to a 2-0 victory over Norwich City at home and there were maximum points at Southampton (2-0) and against Aston Villa (2-0), while he was absent through suspension.

Yet another curling free-kick from Gascoigne, this time past England 'keeper, Peter Shilton, earned Spurs a point against Derby County at the Baseball Ground. More injury problems as he came off at half-time at Highfield Road where Spurs gained another valuable point in a 1-1 draw.

Missing through injury for the tremendous 2-1 victory at Nottingham Forest and a narrow 1-2 defeat with the visit of Liverpool, Gazza returned for the away fixture at Kenilworth Road. A tremendous solo goal by him sealed a convincing 3-1 win over Luton Town.

Tottenham's winning form continued with a 3-0 victory at home to West Ham United, but the visit of Sheffield Wednesday ended goalless. A final flourish saw Wimbledon beaten at Plough Lane 2-1, Everton go down by the same score at The Lane, and Millwall thrashed 5-0 at The Den. Finally, a 1-0 defeat at Queens Park Rangers ended an amazingly roller coaster first season in London for Gazza.

GAZZA FAX

John Gascoigne, Gazza's dad, gave Paul "hell" after he was sent-off for Newcastle at Queens Park Rangers in season 1987-88.

A COMMAND TO GO FORWARD

AT HOME

With Gazza

Home for Gazza is an impressive four-bedroom modern house in a rural corner of Hertfordshire.

The house has touches of a Spanish style villa and sits in an exclusive cul-de-sac where Gazza has already made a big impact on his neighbours.

It is conveniently situated for Paul's first love - fishing. The River Lea flows leisurely along close by, while the Lea Valley itself is well served with an abundance of lakes, pits and trout ponds.

Gazza's home has been furnished to his and his girlfriend Gail's own taste and, for some reason, he has a couple of giant china tigers looking out from the French windows - one munching a Turkish Delight!

But the house contains all the conveniences of modern living and Paul admits that he enjoyed choosing the carpets and furniture and other fittings that say a good deal about his own lively personality.

Yet, although he loves his newly-acquired home, he admits that he does not enjoy spending too much time there. "I'm too hyperactive although I do enjoy a quite drink with Gail," he says. But there are certain times -particularly on the eve of a game - when he must stay in. Even then though, he keeps himself occupied.

"I enjoy watching television and will tune in for any sport that might be on," he says. "I can't stand the soaps - I think they're all useless - but I love a bit of comedy.

"I have no real favourites - maybe Abbott and Costello, Benny Hill and Russ Abbott - but I'll watch anything that is funny."

Gazza admits that he particularly relishes the old clowns and comedians from days gone by. And his music shows a similar hankering back to the days when the personalities themselves were funny rather than the product of a good scriptwriter, and singing artists were less manufactured.

"Elvis Presley is my favourite - I love the King," he says. "He was brilliant, as is Neil Diamond. I don't rate the up-to-date stuff - Harry Secombe could get in the charts these days!

"I'm not really a music fanatic with a massive record collection, but I do listen to tapes or to the radio," he continues. "I play the organ at home and also have a music machine which allows me to sing along with backing tapes."

At this point Gazza launches into "*song*", more like the "*Frogs Chorus*" than the intended "*Love on the Rocks!*" A brief selection of rugby arias does little to enhance his choral reputation!

"I play the organ quite a lot and can belt out a few tunes like "*Eidelweiss*"."

The repertoire is obviously stunning and must have delighted his fellow guests at the hotel that was his home for much of his first year with Tottenham!

"I do have a good laugh and even combine the organ with the record machine to produce my own stuff. Paul Moran and Philip Gray have been in for a singsong but I won't be asking them back!

"I'm not a brilliant singer, as I've just proved, but I enjoy it and that's why I've got all the gear. We have some great laughs."

Gazza admits that he reads little apart from his favourite newspaper, the Sun, and has a gardener to keep his home looking its best. He would love

GAZZA FAX

Gazza admits that former Newcastle manager, Jack Charlton "frightened him to death" when he threatened him with the sack for being overweight.

to have more animals living with him if he could devote more time to them, but contents himself with a couple of Zebra Finches and playing with the giant Burmese Mountain Dog he bought his father, when he returns to Newcastle.

But Paul is a dab hand at DIY and put in half the bathroom at his house. He also describes himself as a "little housewife", and is happy to tidy around although he admits that he hates washing and ironing - he takes that home to his mother!

"I am proud of my home but I would be happy living anywhere," he concludes. "It's much more grand than our old house in Newcastle but that is mainly because I was advised to invest in a home of my own. Yes, it is quite special - but it won't change me in any way.

"What it does allow me to do is entertain my family, Gail's folks, and our friends here at weekends. I love having them here to stay with me. I also have been lucky with my new neighbours - particularly Keith and Sylvia who helped me a lot when I first moved in."

With that, Gazza checked the messages on his answer phone, picked up his fishing rods and set off for the nearby riverbank.

"I live here for many reasons but mainly because of its situation. I am within casting distance of the river, close to Tottenham and Mill Hill. It couldn't be better."

And if he feels hungry, he can always fight the tiger for that Turkish Delight.

Who Inspires Gazza?

Even now, as a 22-year-old England international, Gazza is still inspired by those around him. And no more so than by Liverpool's Republic of Ireland striker, *John Aldridge*.

"I don't know why it is, but he has really caught my eye lately," says Paul. "John works hard and wants success and those are qualities I like in a player.

"*Chris Waddle, Peter Beardsley* and *Bryan Robson* all come into that category. I appreciate a good player but they must have heart.

"These are the sort of players who will inspire the youngsters of today to become the footballers of tomorrow. That inspiration is important but my own encouragement came from other areas because I didn't watch much football as a youngster - I was too busy playing.

"I had help from all along from my father, *John*, from the various boys clubs I played for and from *Colin Suggett* and *Jimmy Nelson* when I started training at Newcastle.

"I am fortunate in that, all along the line, the people that I needed and the inspiration I sought, were there. I can't name them all here because we would need volumes but I am grateful to them all.

"Their help meant that, by the time I turned professional, I had served the best apprenticeship of all."

20 THINGS YOU DIDN'T KNOW ABOUT *Gazza*

1 England's World Cup hope for the future was born on May 27, 1967, 10 months after England's historic victory in that competition.

2 He was only 13 when he first came into contact with England manager Bobby Robson - training with Ipswich Town as a schoolboy.

3 Signed full-time professional forms for Newcastle United in May 1985.

4 Made his first full League appearance for Newcastle at Southampton at the start of the 1985-86 season - his performance earned him a standing ovation from the travelling Geordie fans when he was substituted near the end.

5 Scored his first League goal for United one month later, coming on as a sub against Oxford United.

6 Made his England Under-21 debut against Morocco in the 1987 "Mini" World Cup. Scored in the 2-0 win.

7 Father John sold his pickup van to fund the trip to France to watch this match.

8 His first car was a Mini, bought for £330. Now he has a BMW.

9 Has one brother, Carl, and two sisters, Anna and Lindsay. His mother, Carol, is an inspector at a local glass factory and his father's name is John.

10 Skippered Newcastle United to victory in the 1985 Youth Cup Final. Newcastle beat Watford 4-1 on aggregate.

11 Still likes to watch his old side whenever he is visiting his native North-East.

12 The actor he most admires is funny-man Eddie Murphy.

13 While still at Newcastle, was farmed out to athletics coach Stan Long to sharpen his pace. Was made to run twenty 100 metre sprints with just 60 seconds rest between each burst!

14 Scored 24 goals in 91 League appearances for Newcastle.

15 Made his England debut in the 1-0 win over Denmark in September 1988. He came on as an 85th minute sub for his former Newcastle team-mate, Peter Beardsley.

16 Scored his first international goal in England's 5-0 win over Albania - his third appearance as sub.

17 Made his League debut for Spurs at his old club Newcastle on September 3, 1988 - the match finished 2-2 after Tottenham trailed 2-0 at half-time.

18 Scored his first goal for Spurs in his second match - the 3-2 home defeat by Arsenal.

19 Uncle Ernie James played 22 League games for Portsmouth in the 1920's.

20 Failed all 8 'O' levels he took at school.

GAZZA WORD

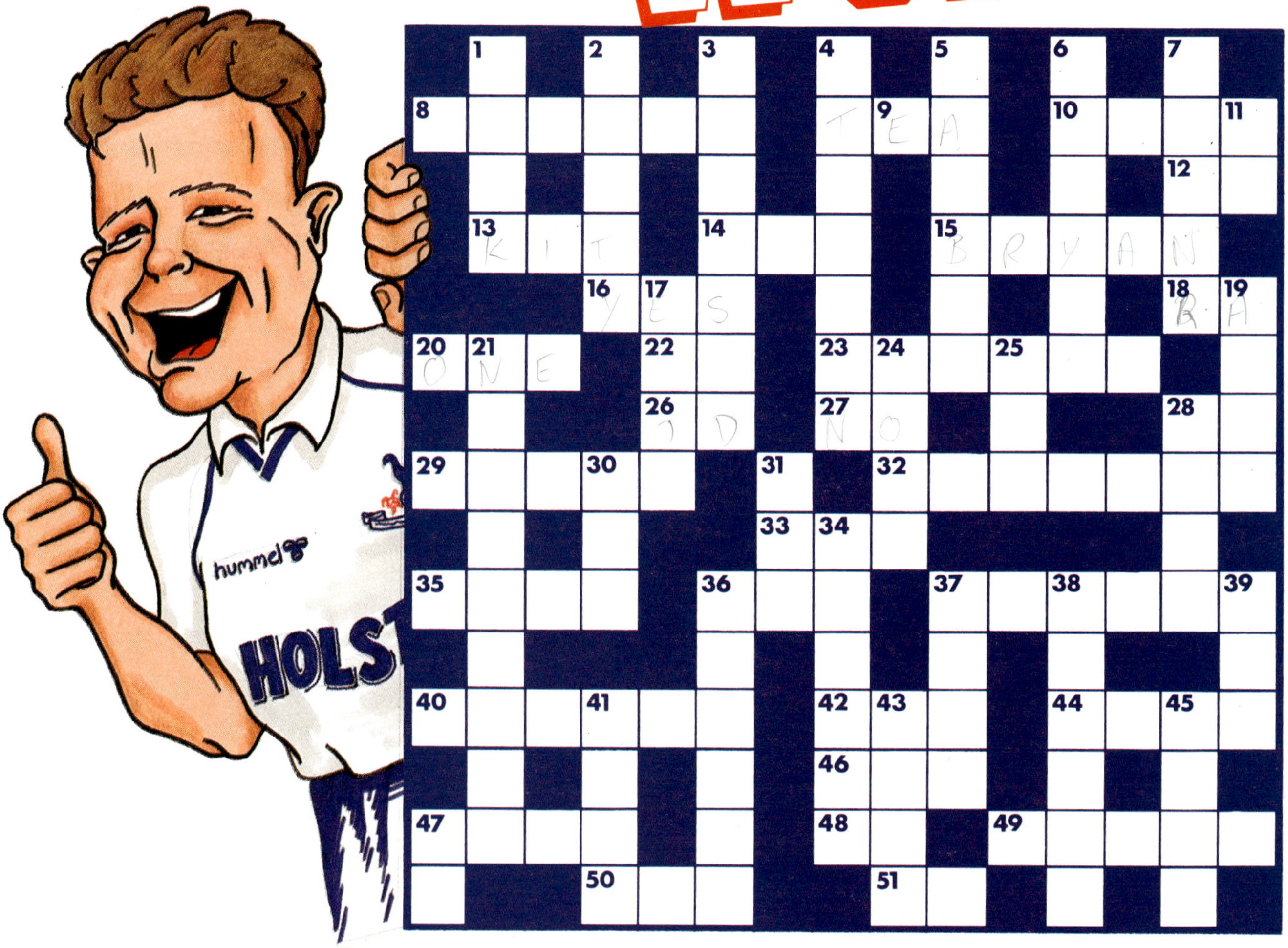

Here's a Gazza-word that is bound to make you 'cross'!

ACROSS

8 Gazza could become one of these (6)
9 Gazza's half-time tipple (3)
10 What Millwall suffered at home to Spurs last season (4)
12 React (2)
13 Playing outfit (3)
14 Fairy (3)
15 First name of Gazza's England leader (5)
16 What Gazza said to Spurs (3)
18 Wishful thinking (2)
20 Gazza's goal tally against Derby last season (3)
22 Venue (2)
23 Mistakes (6)
26 Initials of West Ham full-back (2)
27 Negative reply (2)
28 Initials of one of Gazza's favourite actors (2)
29 What Gazza forces the purists to do (5)
32 Club Gazza scored his first Spurs goal against (7)
33 A Rangers player (3)
35 Final (4)
36 Ray C. . .ence (3)
37 Manufacturers of Gazza's strip (6)
40 Nobby ..... (ex Manchester United and England) (6)
42 Circuit of honour (3)
44 Part of neck (4)
46 Night before (3)
47 .... Ham, where Gazza was injured last season (4)
48 .. Johnson, Scottish international (2)
49 Tony ....., ex England stylist (5)
50 Slip Up (3)
51 ..yim, Gazza's midfield partner (2)

DOWN

1 Spurs 'keeper's first name (4)
2 Celebration (5)
3 Gazza's does this with many goalscorers (7)
4 First name of Coventry 'keeper (7)
5 Challenges Gazza (6)
6 Got one of these when Gazza's on song (6)
7 First name of Gazza's Icelandic team-mate (5)
11 John Pols..n, young Spurs defender (2)
17 Deserve (4)
19 What Gazza enjoys playing (4)
21 Gazza's former club (9)
24 Spurs fans do this when Gazza scores (4)
25 ...ie, former great Spurs midfielder (3)
28 White Hart .... (4)
30 What Gazza can sometimes be - initially (3)
31 Grow old (3)
34 A cockerel is Tottenham's one (6)
36 Medieval joker (5)
37 Wish for best (4)
38 Another Spurs midfielder (6)
39 Fib (3)
41 Delayed (4)
43 Waterway that might attract Gazza (4)
45 Playing area (4)
47 Us (2)

GAZZA FAX

Gazza was voted PFA Young Player of the Year in 1987-88.

POSITION MATCH—UP

Match-up the question numbers with those on the 'pitch' to show you the position of the players in the clues.

1 Plays north of the border for Graeme

2 Young man who made his mark with Spurs last season

3 Sounds Dutch, but plays for Wales and the boys in blue on Merseyside

4 Captains the above at club and national level

5 Leader of the Reds

6 One-time Spurs player, until he returned to Mr Clough

7 England leader, not Bobby

8 ... who else?!

9 Gazza's constant team-mate at Newcastle, Tottenham and for England

10 Young Gunner

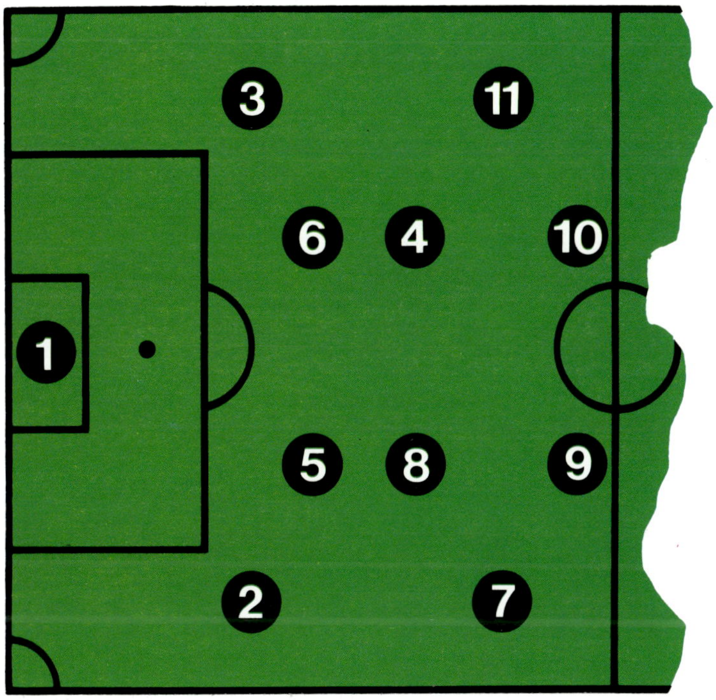

11 One of three brothers who play for Luton

letter-fit

Supply the missing letters to find the name of the footballer.

1 XAX RXSX
2 GXRX LXNXKXR
3 XLXN XOXDXE
4 CXIXE XLXEX
5 XRXCX GXOXBXLXAX
6 CXRXS XAXDXE
7 XEXNX DXLXLXSX
8 GXAXMX SXAXP
9 XEXEX BXAXDXLXY

GAZZA FAX

In one match against Arsenal, Gazza completely dominated Steve Williams and, nipping past him for the 100th time, pulled out an imaginary pocket and said: "You can come out now!"

The Great Gazza FOOTBALL QUIZ

Welcome to the Great Gazza Football Quiz. This is quaranteed to test your football knowledge. Don't back down now, have a go!
Add up your score and we will tell you just how good you are!
The answers are on pages 60-61.

1 Where did Tottenham play their home matches before moving to White Hart Lane? 1point

2 Who scored the first ever World Cup goal? 1point

3 What Brazilian club did Pele make famous? 1point

4 Who will stage the 1990 World Cup Finals? 1point

5 Who was the winner of the 1989 FA Cup and what was the score? 2 points

6 Who is the captain of the England team? 1point

7 From which Argentine club did Spurs sign Osvaldo Ardiles? 1point

8 Which current test cricketer once played for Scunthorpe United? 1point

9 How many England caps has Emlyn Hughes won? 1point

10 Who, in 1986, became the first African nation to get beyond the first round of the World Cup Finals? 1point

11 Against what team did Gazza score his first goal for Tottenham Hotspur? What was the final score? 2 points

12 Against what international team did Gazza score his first goal for England? What was the final score? 2 points

13 How many times have Newcastle won the Football League Championship? 1point

14 Who was the top goalscorer in the 1986 World Cup Finals? 1point

15 Which nations have won the World Cup three times? 1point

16 What famous teams play at these eight grounds? 8 points

a. Ibrox Stadium
b. Highbury
c. Goodison Park
d. Anfield Road
e. The Den
f. Old Trafford
g. Kenilworth Road
h. Stamford Bridge

0-5 **Please tell me you're joking! Football, you know - the game where you try to kick a ball into a net!**

6-10 **Perhaps you meant to buy a book on gardening!**

11-15 **Alright. Maybe you've had a bad day. Read through this Annual again and have another 'attempt'.**

16-20 **Not bad, not bad at all, I'm impressed.**

21-27 **CHEAT!**

FACE MATCH

There are 4 football celebrities below, but they have been mixed up with each other. Do you know who the 4 are?

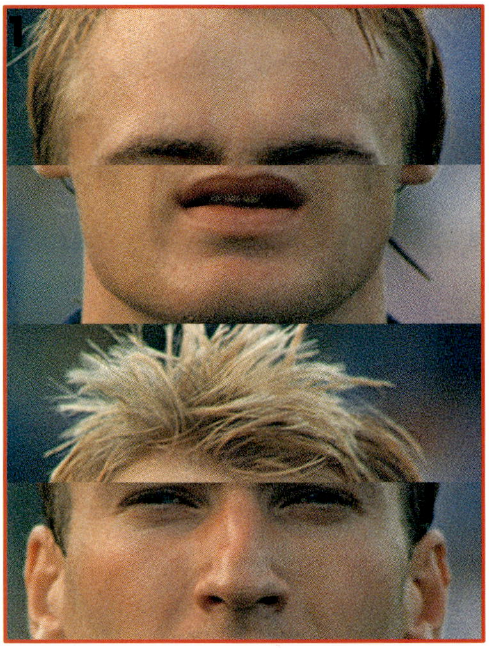

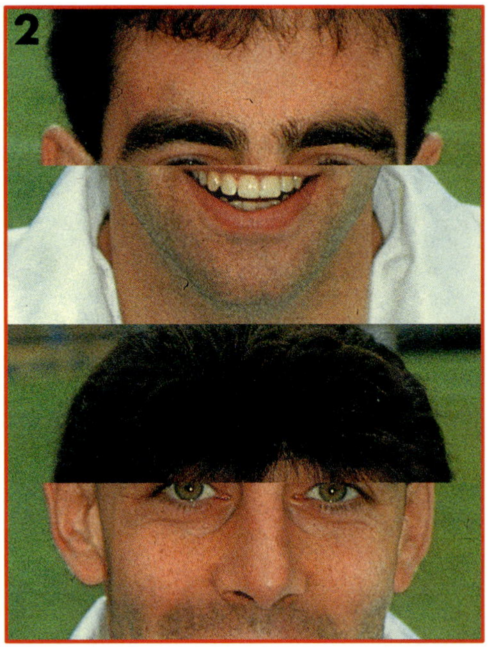

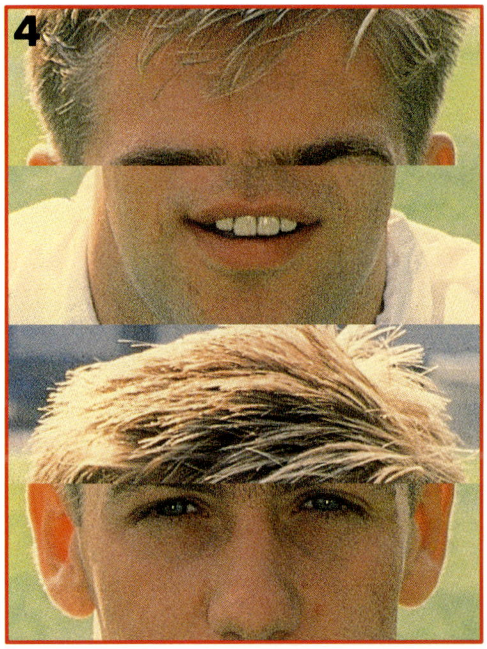

Ball Logic

Study the sequence of numbers, then work out logically the next number.

1

GAZZA FAX

Before England's 5-0 World Cup qualifier defeat of Albania, manager Bobby Robson described his talented young player as being "daft as a brush". At training next day, Gazza turned up with a brush stuck down his stocking!

FOOTBALL

. . . . was the thing for me

It is difficult to imagine what Gazza would be if he was not a top class footballer. Because he is definitely not suited to anything else!

Schooldays saw him sitting bored to tears as he gazed from the classroom dreaming of an escape to the playground or, even better, for the weekly sports sessions to come round.

By the time he reached Secondary School, the young Gascoigne was convinced that he would make it as a footballer. Indeed, he had no ambition in any other direction and tended to see other subjects as distractions from his ultimate goal.

"School wasn't too bad but I really only enjoyed it when we had PE," he recalls. "I hated History and Maths and such subjects and at those times all I wanted to do was to get out into the fresh air.

"I did pass English,Maths and Environmental Studies at CSE level but I wasn't too bothered because, by then, I was already at Newcastle United.

"In fact, I can't even tell you what my class mates went on to do because all my friends by then were footballers. I was single-minded about my football and I lost touch with all the others at school."

Gazza spent every waking hour playing football and so never even worked part-time as a youngster. While others sought summer and Saturday jobs to earn extra money, Gazza refused to allow such distractions to interfere with his football.

"I never had a job of any sort," he says. "I had my pocket money of between 30-50p but I didn't need much. In fact, for the most part, I had no money whatsoever as a child but it didn't bother me one bit then and it doesn't bother me now."

Gazza's father, John, worked as a labourer but illness forced him to stop although, fortunately, that is all behind him now. His mother's name is Carol; he has one brother, Carl, and two sisters, Anna and Lindsay.

Gazza's success has meant that he has been able to buy his parents and his sisters a house apiece and also purchase his father a BMW. Obviously his family must play an important part in his life?

"Yes, they matter very much to me," says Gazza with feeling. "When I retire I will, hopefully, have enough money to be secure myself and to enable me to look after them. Thankfully I'm doing all right and I'm well looked after by the people around me."

How does he see the future? Would he like to stay in the game after he finishes his playing career?

"At the moment I am just 22 and I have no plans as yet," he says. "In five to seven years time I will start looking to the future but I've really only just started out.

"If I wasn't a footballer I reckon that I would be doing nothing. Obviously I would be looking around the factories back home in Newcastle for some sort of job but I know that I would hate it and wouldn't be any good at it. As a result, I would either leave or get the sack.

"I feel sorry for people who, through no fault of their own, find themselves in that position. I've been fortunate and I'm thankful for that.

"I always wanted to be a professional footballer - I was never interested in anything else and that feeling remains today."

How the FOOTBALL WORLD sees Gazza

England manager Bobby Robson on Gazza's dazzling contribution as substitute in the 5-0 win against Albania:
"I enjoyed some of the things he did. But you need two balls when he plays, one for him and another for the rest of us! I liked some of his dribbles - when he almost got into the box it was like watching George Best. I've been in the game a long time and I've never met anyone with more confidence than this kid."

Former Manchester United and Northern Ireland legend George Best:
"Gascoigne is the one player in the country who oozes class consistently. He is a fantastic player - the sort the public wants to see.
"There's no doubt he has the chance to be a big star, though there is more pressure on him than I had in my time."

Liverpool goalkeeper Bruce Grobbelaar:
"I sometimes wonder whether he is trying to emulate our Great Dane by getting as big as Jan Molby - he's about 15 stone!
"Having said that, he is probably the most skilful young midfield player in the country. He has so much flair and confidence. Gazza creates many good chances out of nothing - he scores spectacular goals and the fans love him. He reminds me of Billy Bremner or Johnny Giles...but with more skill than either of them."

Late Newcastle manager, Joe Harvey, sometimes saw, *"touches of Len Shackleton in him."*

GAZZA FAX

Gazza's most cherished articles of clothing: his boxer shorts ... like him, they are very colourful!

The irrepressible Tommy Docherty:

"He has a great image with the media. With some improvement he could go all the way!"

Liverpool and England midfielder Steve McMahon:

"He is a very intelligent player, he likes to take control of the ball in commanding positions from where he can distribute it to his team-mates.

"He seems to enjoy getting involved in the action and playing short, neat passes rather than sweeping, crossfield ones. He also likes to by-pass people by playing a lot of tricky one-twos."

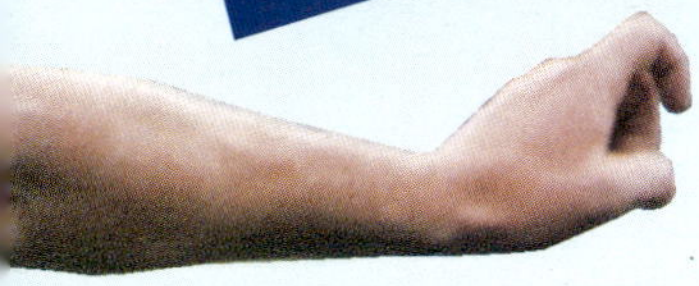

West Ham's long-serving Billy Bonds after an engaging midfield duel:

"If you take away his competitive edge you will destroy him. We had about a dozen tackles together and a couple of little tussles, and there was no trouble at all. He's hard, but fair, and that's all you could want of anybody."

Gazza's former Newcastle manager, Willie McFaul:

"Self-discipline is what Paul needs most of all. With it, the world can be his oyster; without it, who knows where he will be in four or five years from now?"

Peter Kirkley, Newcastle's youth development officer, recalls how Gazza was "small and dumpy" when he first spotted him as a 13-year-old:

"He was a bit of a plodder, but controlled the ball beautifully. Even at that age he had a certain arrogance."

Gazza's D-I-Y Coaching Session

If Paul Gascoigne has a secret formula for turning a schoolboy into a soccer star, then he is keeping it to himself. He struggles to put his finger on what separates him from the many thousands who fall by the wayside each year.

And Gazza is no ordinary footballer. Indeed, he is considered by most to be the outstanding young talent of our day in this country. So how did he do it?

"My earliest memories are receiving a football from my father for my seventh birthday and going into the park with it to play with my mates," he says. "We played all the time and I certainly had no interest in anything else.

"I wasn't one of those lads who practised all day against a wall or worked on particular routines. But those games at home took me through every aspect of the game and if I did discover a skill or what I considered to be a good move I would work on it.

"In fact, I was so happy playing in those games with the other lads, that I hardly watched a match as a youngster. I was only interested in playing all the time and my father and brother would join in when I needed an opponent.

"So what would I advise youngsters today? Get a ball and get into the park. Either that or win the pools!

"I would tell them to learn something and then practice it. When you've mastered that, move on to the next one. That old adage about practice making perfect is very true and there are no short cuts.

"I loved the likes of Johann Cruyff and Pele as a kid but although they had incredible natural talent they still had to work at it. You have nothing if you can't apply your skills consistently in a game."

Gazza did not see a professional match until the age of 12 when he watched Newcastle reserves in action and then, at the age of 15, saw the first team play just once. But by then he was already part of the setup at St. James's Park having gone there when just 12, becoming an Associated Schoolboy at 14 and an apprentice two years later.

"It all meant that I did not watch much football because I was playing myself," he explains.

GAZZA FAX

Gazza is not a renowned tipster. Before Wimbledon's shock FA Cup Final victory, he said: "I can't see Liverpool failing." Of course, a Lawrie Sanchez header ensured that the mighty Reds did!

Gazza's D-I-Y Coaching Session

At that time, the young Gazza was greatly sought after. He trained with Ipswich Town under present-day England boss, Bobby Robson, and was wanted by Southampton and Middlesbrough. But he had no wish to leave home nor to go anywhere apart from his beloved Newcastle United.

Who did he admire as a kid? "Just myself - I didn't see anybody else," laughs Gazza. Then a bit of political crawling. "I was impressed with Terry Venables as a player - I thought to myself, one day I'll play for him!"

But once he started his apprenticeship at Newcastle, Gazza found an instant hero - the great Kevin Keegan who recently invited Gazza back to St. James's Park, along with Spurs team-mate, Chris Waddle, to play in his side in a testimonial game.

"I was Keegan's apprentice and used to clean his boots," recalled Gazza. "Kevin was a world class player and I was just pleased to be assigned to him."

Once he forced his way into the Newcastle first-team as a 17-year-old, Gazza was immediately impressed by a whole host of midfielders who opposed him. And one was his Spurs predecessor, Glenn Hoddle.

"I like good players in any position and, at that age, saw a good many that I wanted to emulate. Manchester United and England skipper, Bryan Robson, is one player that I really admired while Glenn impressed me very much whenever we played Tottenham.

"It is ironic that I should follow him to Spurs but I was never worried when people described me as the new Hoddle at the time of my move. You can't complain at comparisons with players of his class, but I am Paul Gascoigne and a different type of player. I'm only interested in being myself.

"Glenn, like Cruyff and Pele, was born with a special talent but, as I say, without working on it, all three would have been nothing. So get that ball and get out there. That's what I'll be doing!"

HOLSTEN

GONE FISHING *OR* SHOOTING

Gazza is a real country boy at heart. He lives close to the River Lea in Hertfordshire and backs on to a neighbour who sells shotguns for a living!

In such an environment - and with a good deal of spare time on his hands - it is not surprising that the two great loves of his life at the moment are shooting and fishing.

Unfortunately, he has not found the fishing in the London area anywhere near as good as that he enjoyed in the countryside surrounding his native Newcastle. But a clay pigeon is a clay pigeon no matter where it is.

"To be fair to London, I haven't had too much time to look, but you don't have to search all that long to find a good spot back home," says Gazza.

"But I just love fishing. It's relaxing and you don't get pestered , because when I set off with my rod and line I like to get well away from it all.

"I loved fishing as a child but I've only been doing it seriously for the past couple of years. I also enjoy sea fishing but when I'm on dry land I'm only interested in fly fishing - course fishing is, in my opinion, a waste of time.

"You sit there, wait for a fish and, if you're lucky enough for it to bite, you reel it in...and chuck it back. Fly fishing is an art. You work for that fish, you need skill to land it and if you catch a fish, you keep it to eat. That's a logical exercise to me.

"It's more of a challenge and I have great memories of fishing on the River Tweed. What a beautiful place to spend your time. The fishing is great and the countryside beautiful."

Every fisherman has his fishing story. Normally it revolves around the proverbial "one that got away", or great deeds in landing a whopper. Gazza's fishing tale concerns...a frog!

He explains: "I was float fishing for trout with my Newcastle teammate, Glenn Roeder, when he nipped off to get the coffees. As I sat on the bank a frog swam by, so I grabbed it, reeled in Glenn's line, tied it to the frog's leg and cast it out again.

"Glenn saw the float bobbing and came sprinting back shouting 'I've got a bite!' He couldn't believe it when he pulled it back and his face was a picture. I just rolled about laughing and the frog, who like Glenn had the hump by then, swam off to warn his mates that there was a nutter on the bank!"

And shooting? "That's another great sport - I love it because it is a great challenge. I'm not interested in static or unrewarding pastimes.

"I've done a lot of clay pigeon shooting - and even went with Wimbledon's Vinny Jones, who is famous for that photograph of him grabbing me by the wotsits in one particular game!

"But I've got no funny stories about shooting. It's a serious business that can be made dangerous by messing around. When I go shooting I concentrate on that alone. There's no scope for joking - even with an air pistol."

GAZZA FAX

After Liverpool had trounced Newcastle 4-0 in December 1987, Gazza chose to take the train home on his own rather than travel on the team coach.

GAZZA THE HOT SHOT

Using any of the numbered clay pigeons above - how many sums, with a toal of 21, can you make? You can only use a clay pigeon once in each sum.

GASCOIGNE

How many words can you make from the 9 letter word - Gascoigne? Maybe you can beat me. I found 46, but over 30 is a score to shout about.

GAZZA FAX

John Gascoigne, spotting his son's potential at an early stage, lied about Paul's age to get him into Redheugh Boys Club, Gateshead, where they had a reputation for producing League players.

Guess The Fish?

Guess the fish by following the clues.

1. A fish that sounds as if it would ***park*** backwards.
2. A fish with large jaws.
3. No ***doubt*** this fish would rhyme.
4. A fish that might swim in the deepest notes.
5. The biggest fish in the sea.
6. A musical fish that can sing a .....
7. Gazza wishes he ***had docks*** full of these.
8. A precious metal fish.
9. A fish you might find at the bottom of your shoe.
10. A galloping fish.

Answers on pages 60-61.

CLAY PIGEON SHOOT

Working from left to right, follow the sequence of the clay pigeons to find out what size and colour pigeon Gazza will shoot next.

'PLAY IT AGAIN' Gazza

As you already know one of Gazza's hobbies is playing the organ. In this puzzle Gazza has played a tune, but which key did he start on?

The numbers indicate how many keys left or right he moved to play the next key, i.e. 4L - 4 keys left, 3R - 3 keys right. If the red cross marks the last key he played, what key did he play first? Each key is only played once.

Here is a clue if you are in trouble. He played the 3R white key second to last, which landed him on the X key. Now find a key with the number and direction that lands you on 2R white, and so on. Until you have only one key left - the first key!

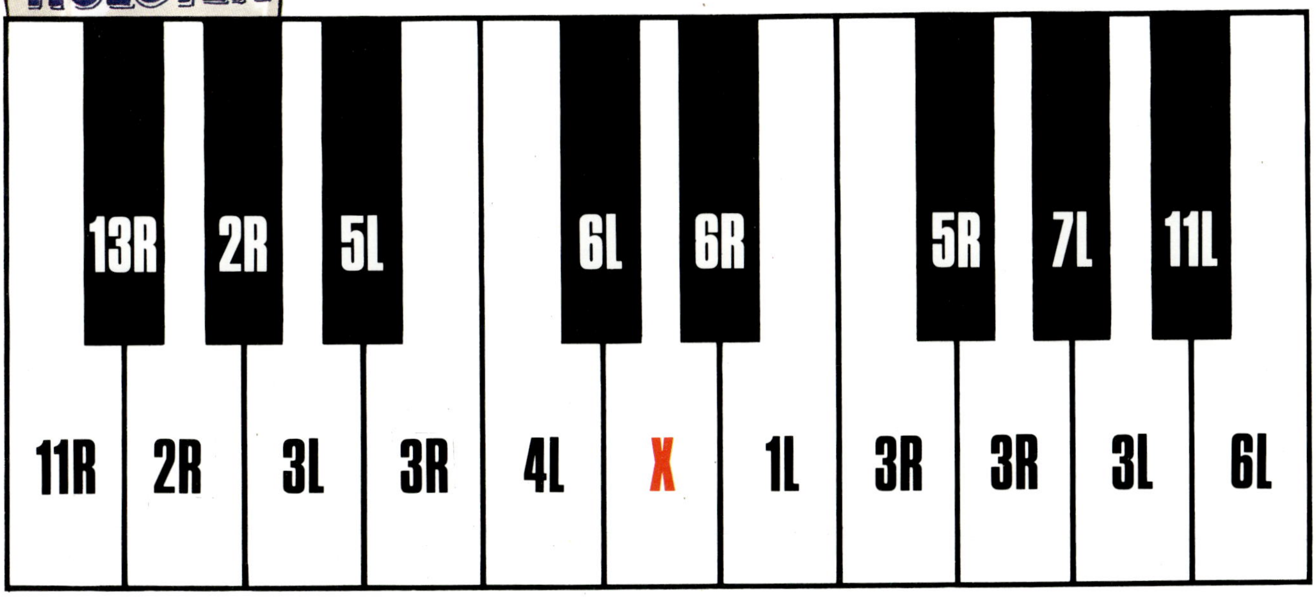

Gazza's Gallery

Photos by:

Bob Thomas and Monte Fresco

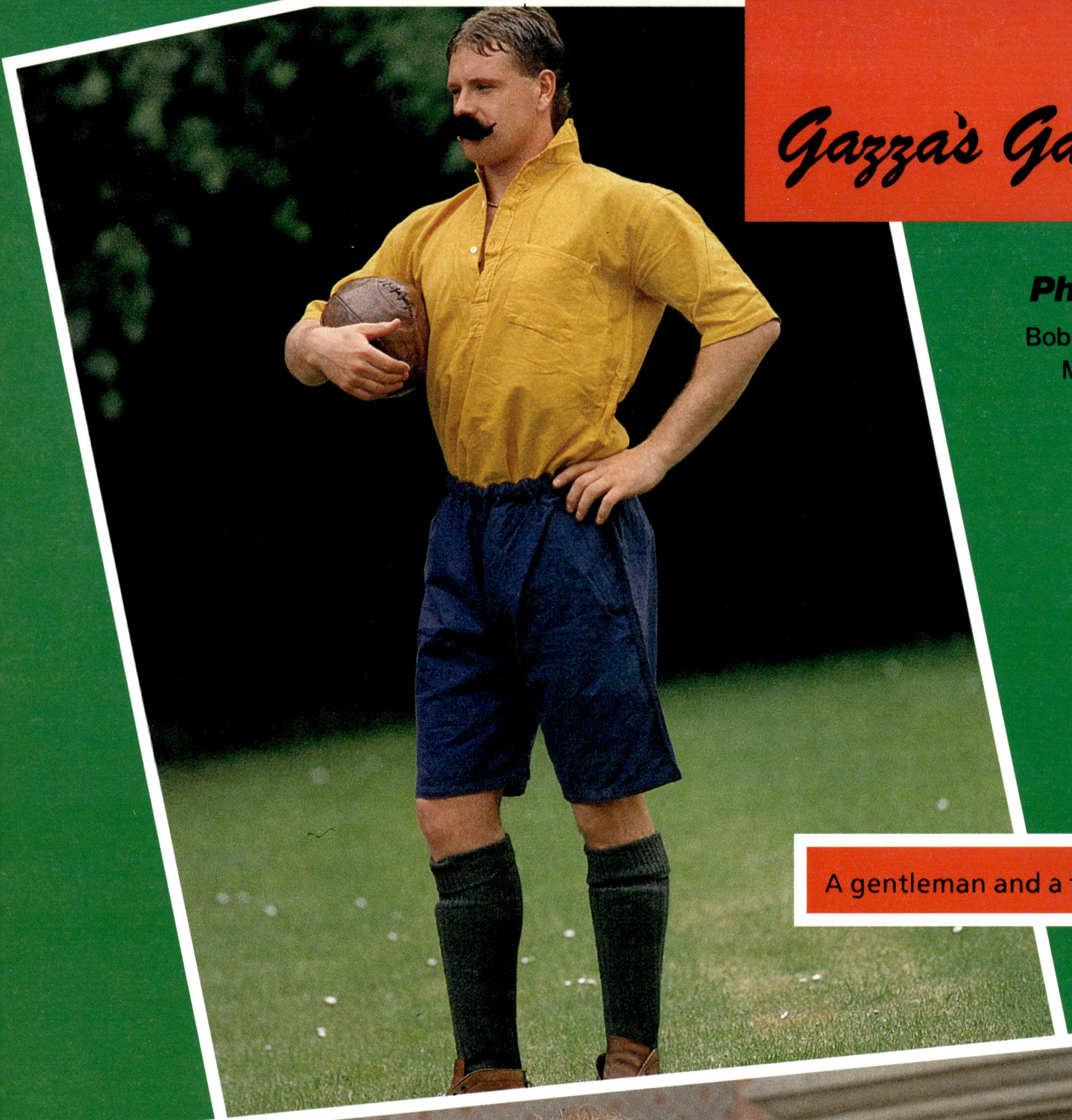

A gentleman and a footballer.

Keep cool

And shoot straight.

Gazza's Gallery

Whatever the weapon, you can rely on the shooting power of Gazza!

LIFE *in* LONDON

"Look at that - exactly what I hate about London!" That was Gazza's summing up as we drove on the M25 towards the venue for the interview.

"Silly old idiots sit in the outside lane doing 60 mph while others cruise in the middle lane. Then, when you're waiting to get past, another nutter overtakes you on the inside.

"That sort of lunatic driving - plus the incessant traffic - is the biggest difference I find between London and Newcastle."

All this and I hadn't even asked him the question yet! What other changes, while we're on the subject, had he noted between the capital and the city of his birth, since he moved south in the summer of 1988?

"There's not really that much - not in the areas that interest me," he answers. "Obviously there would be if I was into night-clubbing, but I don't need that sort of thing so life remains very much the same for me.

"I used to go home to see my family and friends every weekend but now that I have got my own house I'm just as likely to relax and have a nice quite weekend with Gail.

"What I miss about Newcastle is that it is easier to get to my fishing and the fact that I know the place so well. I also miss my family and my mates. It's not bad where I'm living but I do get lonely easily and that gets to me sometimes.

"London's got quite a lot to offer but you have to go out of your way to get people to talk to you down here. I'm also not interested in the theatre - I'd rather be fishing in any weather - so really, as I don't go into town much, you should be asking me the difference between Hertfordshire, where I now live, and Newcastle. I don't think I could stand living in Central London!

"One thing the area has to offer is a lot of good restaurants and I do enjoy a good meal with Gail and good company. And one other advantage is that I can go out for a drink without anybody recognising me and that allows me to relax more. I can come and go as I please which is a great change.

"But the pace of life in London is very fast. I don't think anybody has got time for anybody else and that's quite a culture shock after the easy-going North-East."

GAZZA FAX

When pint-sized referee, Alan Seville, complained of a headache once, Gazza called to the bench: "Have we got any Junior Disprin?"

A TYPICAL DAYS *training*

MONDAY

"Normally the day to get the weekend out of our systems," says Gazza. "Much depends on how we did on the Saturday, but, no matter what, we still have a light session. We have a chat, loosen up and then start looking forward to the next game. If it's a midweek match, then we will probably do a little bit more."

Throwing ice, hiding articles of other players' clothing, making joke calls to the coinbox on his mobile telephone...all fit into the typical training day routine for Gazza, the self-confessed nutcase.

But when it comes to the actual training - Gazza is ready to work as hard as the most determined player at White Hart Lane.

On average, he is rarely out of bed before 8.45am and after getting himself ready he departs to Chase Lodge, Mill Hill, where training normally starts at around 10.30am.

"The training routine all depends on what the manager has planned," explains Gazza. "We warm up for around 20 minutes with the Assistant Manager and then Terry Venables will put us through our paces."

That routine, as Gazza explains, depends very much on how the games are going and if there are certain aspects that need improving on. But this is how the average week goes for Gazza and his Spurs team - mates.

TUESDAY

"This is always a tough day. We work on set pieces, working against defenders and such but if we have a match on the Wednesday, then we do ease off on the graft. But, normally, it is a day for hard work."

Gazza adores eating not Mars Bars, as continually claimed, but Crunchies.

GAZZA FAX

WEDNESDAY

"Again, it is difficult to be precise because so much depends on midweek games and how we are doing on the field. If we are going to have a day off, this will be it, but if we are not playing well and there is work to be done, then this can be another hard day."

THURSDAY

"I normally enjoy Thursdays because this is when we might have a practice game and that is what I like most. By then we will have formulated our approach to Saturday's game and will put it to the test against the Reserves on the training field. And make no mistake, these are hard games because all the players in the Reserves want to catch the manager's eye and this is a great opportunity for them. Sometimes they are asked to play in a particular way to imitate Saturday's opposition but, like us, they are out there to win and, with the strength in depth at Tottenham, they are well capable of it."

FRIDAY

"After a good warm up, we often have a brief mini-game but little else. By now all our concentration and energies are focused on that kick-off on Saturday."

SATURDAY

"My match day routine rarely changes but obviously is a key aspect of my life. Match days are long, often draining affairs but they are what it is all about. A full breakdown of a typical match day can be found elsewhere in this book."

SUNDAY

"Normally, we have Sunday off and I can take things easy at home and got out fishing or visiting friends. But there are times when we have to train on a Sunday and you have to accept that as part of a footballer's life.A bad run - particularly if we have a midweek game - can force us in on a Sunday. In fact, it's not that unusual to train on Christmas Day!"

GAZZA FAX

Gazza would like to meet the Queen, just to ask what she thinks of Saint and Greavsie!

Adds Gazza: "I love training. I look forward to going in every morning and enjoy all aspects of the various routines. We don't do too much stamina work in midweek once the season is underway because we have to keep our strength for the game itself, but even when we do, I'm happy to do it.

"Fitness is the platform you must reach before you can do anything else in football and has to be a prerequisite of any footballer. You are nothing if you can't compete for the full 90 minutes. So I'm happy to work hard on improving my stamina and it leaves me raring to go by the time the game comes around.

"Training days are different at Spurs and Newcastle, with some aspects having more priority over others at the two clubs. I don't want to say too much and give away the Tottenham secret but I will say that I find it more varied and interesting under Terry Venables.

"After the session finishes, I often stay on and practice my shooting against goalkeeper Erik Thorstvedt, who enjoys the extra workout himself.

"But I'm not too sure how long that's going to go on. After our last session, I pinched his underpants and he had to go home without any. God knows what his missus thought! Until now, he didn't know who did it but if you are reading this, Erik mate, you can have them back - if I can find them!

"He probably had an idea who nicked his pants but I'll have to watch my back now! But Erik's a great bloke and he's getting used to all the larking about and wind-ups that go on. He called us the "Crazy Gang" when he first arrived at Tottenham but he's resigned to it all now - even if it's a bit drafty going home sometimes!"

SPOT THE DIFFERENCE

In the two cartoons below there are 15 hidden differences - can you find them? Sounds easy, but I wouldn't be too smug if I were you!

GAZZA FAX

At Newcastle Gazza played football in the local parks with scores of 12-year-olds to help him keep fit.

WORLD CUP

How many words can you make from the 8 letter word - World Cup? Maybe you can beat me! I found 18, but over 10 is a score to be proud of.

Can you draw these circles without lifting your pen off the page and without repeating any of the lines?

Welcome to Team Search, a puzzle within a puzzle.
Hidden in the word search below are the names of 20 football teams. When you have found them match 12 of the teams with the 12 football club logos around the outside.

So here are the 20 football teams:-

Arsenal, Aston Villa, Bristol Rovers, Cardiff City, Celtic, Charlton Athletic, Chelsea, Derby County, Everton, Leeds United, Liverpool, Luton Town, Manchester United, Millwall, Norwich City, Sheffield Wednesday, Southampton, Tottenham Hotspur, West Ham United and Wimbledon.

TEAM SEARCH

A	I	H	B	G	O	C	L	T	D	Y	O	E	Y	T	C	C	F
C	U	S	N	O	R	W	I	C	H	C	I	T	Y	B	A	H	Y
I	M	E	V	E	R	T	O	N	C	H	N	O	T	R	R	A	R
T	S	A	L	U	T	O	N	T	O	W	N	A	D	I	D	R	I
M	O	V	N	L	I	V	C	I	U	E	T	E	Y	S	I	L	I
T	U	T	L	C	H	E	L	S	E	A	T	L	E	T	F	T	Y
P	T	A	T	C	H	U	E	Y	T	I	C	N	M	O	F	O	N
D	H	R	R	E	S	E	T	E	N	V	D	N	A	L	C	N	O
E	A	S	O	L	N	O	S	U	Y	E	D	L	F	R	I	A	C
R	M	E	T	T	Y	H	M	T	W	E	L	I	O	O	T	T	T
B	P	N	H	I	C	A	A	D	E	I	L	V	R	V	Y	H	I
Y	T	A	C	C	H	M	L	M	V	R	M	E	E	E	O	L	Y
C	O	L	A	T	H	E	E	N	H	C	U	B	S	R	F	E	O
O	N	L	S	I	I	N	O	D	S	O	A	N	L	S	Y	T	U
U	T	E	T	F	I	T	E	O	L	O	T	U	I	E	T	I	C
N	W	I	F	O	S	H	A	M	C	O	U	S	N	T	D	C	P
T	P	E	L	A	M	I	L	L	W	A	L	L	P	Y	E	O	T
Y	H	L	I	V	E	R	P	O	O	L	W	E	S	U	T	D	N
S	A	E	V	L	E	E	D	S	U	N	I	T	E	D	R	L	Y

Gazza's Gallery

Opposition? Make 'em laugh.....

Or carry them off!

Short Term Ambitions?

To Win Everything!

When Paul Gascoigne moved south to Tottenham from Newcastle United in the summer of 1988, he took with him one main ambition. He badly wanted to win a League Championship medal with his new club.

A year later, that desire burns as fiercely as ever. Only now Gazza wants to add a World Cup Winners' medal to the collection of his dreams.

His response is instant when questioned about those immediate ambitions.

"I want Tottenham to win the League and, in doing so, prove all those clever people wrong who say that it is beyond us," insists Paul. "Everybody expected us to finish below the top 10 last season but we could have made it to the leading three if we hadn't had such a bad start.

"I can't wait to see what next season brings now."

Gazza was talking before the 1988-89 campaign had even finished and there is no doubt that his will be an even more consistent and valuable contribution with a season at White Hart Lane under his belt.

He needed time to gel with his new team-mates and when you have the role of the play-maker the urgency for the bedding-in period to be completed rapidly can be more acute. The same could be applied to the England international side but, at both levels, there are clear signs that Gazza is winning the battle. "I'm proud to play for Spurs - and for England," he says. "My Spurs debut, ironically at Newcastle, and my first goal - against Arsenal - were magical moments as was the time I pulled on that England shirt. Just picking that kit up was great - I really loved it.

"Scoring for England against Albania at Wembley was another great feeling. I just couldn't believe it when that goal went in because it is every youngster's dream to do just that. What a setting for your first goal. Now I want a hat-trick!

"Just playing for England matters to me because this is my country and I want us to be the best. I'll tell you what, it was the best feeling I ever had when I walked out on that pitch for the warm up, and I looked up and saw my Dad sitting there in the stand. That was brilliant - it brought a lump to my throat.

"And just being a part of such a tremendous squad can only help make you a better player.

"So I want England to win the World Cup and Spurs to lift the title. Don't bet against either. Both are quite possible when you look at the players involved."

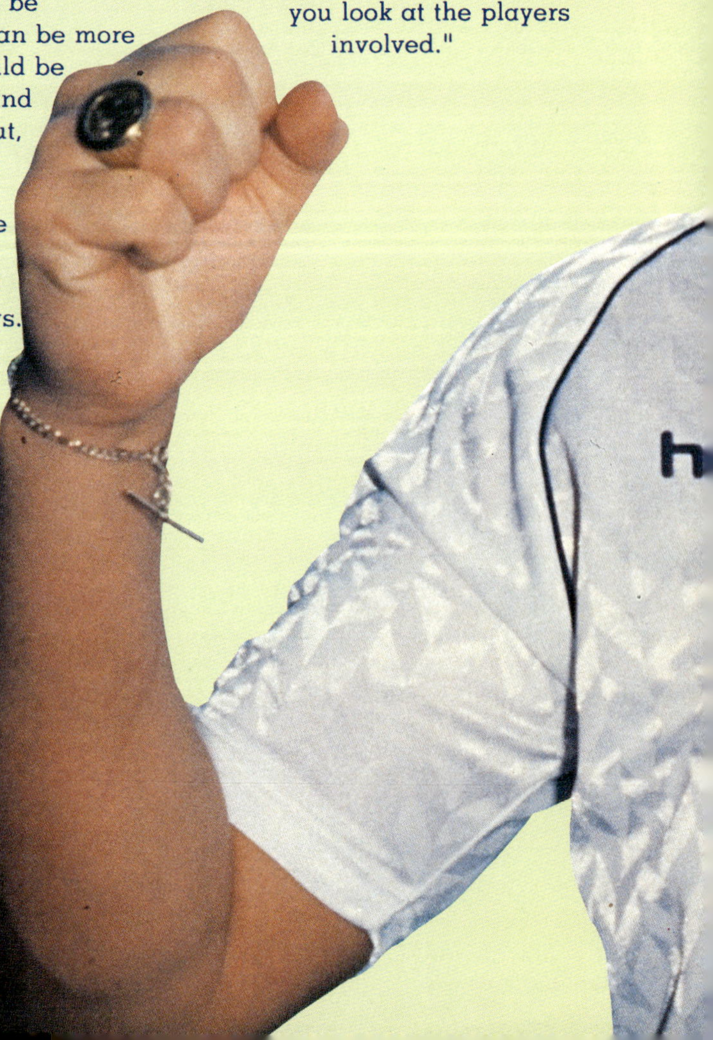

"When you are 16 or so, you look at England on television and wonder what it would be like to play at that level. Well I've been there and done it and hopefully it will inspire today's youngsters to hear me say that it's brilliant. You've got to go for it if you've got the chance.

GAZZA FAX

Gazza made his 100th League appearance in Tottenham's 2-1 home defeat by Southampton on October 25, 1988.

A *typical* MATCH DAY

There was a knock on the referee's dressing room door. There stood Gazza completely covered in bandages.

You've gotta give me more protection, Ref," begged the mummified Gazza through a split in the strapping covering his head with just eye holes remaining.

That scenario actually happened at White Hart Lane after another bruising encounter last season. But although there was a serious side to the situation, Gazza - true to form - played it for laughs.

"I did get a bit of a kicking that day but I couldn't get the referee to respond," recalls Gazza. "It was also around the time that manager Terry Venables had appealed in the newspapers for officials to clamp down on the type of play that was driving the positive things from our game, so I thought I would have a joke.

"I borrowed all the bandages from our physio, John Sheridan, and the referee couldn't believe it when I walked in like Boris Karloff. But he had a good laugh - even if I'm still getting kicked in games!"

Gazza enjoys a good exchange of views with the unfortunate referee during a game and that has become very much a part of his match day routine.

"I said to one in one match: 'Here, Ref, what would you do if I called you a plonker?' He said: 'I'd book you.' So I said: 'What would you do if I thought you were a plonker?' He said: 'Nothing.' I said: 'Well I think you're a plonker then, Ref!

"Then there was the time that West Ham veteran, Billy Bonds, was lying on the ground waiting for the physio. I said: 'Here, Billy, I hope it's not a

touch of arthritis.' I won't say what his reply was!"

There can be no doubt that Gazza revels in the atmosphere of a match day. Yet the jokes and leg-pulls are slotted in and around a regular routine. He describes his typical Saturday:

"The Friday night before is a time to get a video and just sit quietly to watch a film. Or I might pop over to see Chris Waddle for a meal at his house.

"I'm up the following morning at 9.30am and just walk about doing nothing. I then have a bath, put my suit on and get ready. I like to leave for a game about 12.30pm and, depending on traffic, arrive at White Hart Lane at around 1.15pm.

"By then I will have had my pre-match meal - either chicken or cornflakes - at home or at a restaurant, but I never eat breakfast.

"I go straight into the dressing room where manager Terry Venables tells us the team and then it's a question of sorting out tickets and relaxing in front of the television in the

Gazza reads The Beano and The Dandy comics.

GAZZA FAX

Players' Lounge before we start getting ready.

"We all crack a few jokes in the dressing room to get everybody in a good humour before the game and we go out for a warm up at about 2.25pm. I normally do a few stretches and sprints and get a good feel of the ball by taking a few shots at Erik. He then retrieves them from the crowd!

"I go back in around 2.45pm, get my shinpads on and Terry reminds us what he wants us to do at specific situations - like the wall and such - during a game. Then the bell goes and we're on our way out.

"I don't have any real superstitions or routines, but I don't like walking up the tunnel in fourth place and I always carry a ball so that I can continue my warm up.

"I always enjoy a game and don't think that the referees get too fed up with my perpetual banter. We seem to have a good rapport.

"At half-time, I have a cup of tea or a glucose drink while Terry talks to us. Then the bell goes again and it's back out and on with the business.

"By the end, I'm too shattered to do much. I just sit down and take it easy while I take my gear off. The mood at that time is always dictated by the result. Naturally I hate losing, but even when that happens, I try to quickly snap out of it and look forward to the next one.

"After a good soak in the bath, I normally stay in the dressing room for a while to allow things to ease a little bit in the lounges. You can't relax when they're packed so I take my time and emerge when people have started to drift away home and things have started to settle down.

"On a Saturday evening, I'm happy with a white wine or a lager in my local. I'm not interested in going out for a meal or going up town. A quiet pint will do me and one of the benefits of life in the London area is that I can do that without being recognised. I couldn't do that in Newcastle because they are all fanatics up there and, although they are great people, there are times when you just want to wind down.

"At away matches, my routine is similar although we nearly always stay at a hotel on the Friday night for games outside London. Even then, my morning preparations are the same - eating at noon and getting to the ground soon after 1pm. But we have some laughs on the coach home - particularly if we've won - and that helps me unwind.

"We pick up our cars from the training ground and then often go for a drink together. I love being with the rest of the lads and if we've won and we've got the following day off, I couldn't be happier."

SPOT THE BALL

Place a cross where you think the ball is.

That's Logic!

Study the sequence of numbers, then work out logically the next number.

6 9 13 16 20 ?

11 13 17 25 32 ?

20 22 26 34 41 ?

GAZZA FAX

Gazza was so intrigued when Brazilian striker, Mirandinha, arrived at Newcastle that he took it upon himself to act as his interpreter at training sessions.

Gazza's COMPETITION

WIN A DAY OUT AT WHITE HART LANE AS THE GUEST OF PAUL GASCOIGNE

Answer the 4 simple questions below, fill in the tie-breaker and you've a great chance of winning a visit to White Hart Lane to watch Tottenham Hotspur in action. First prize is two tickets to one of Spurs' home matches as the VIP guest of Paul Gascoigne and the club. The day will include a tour of the ground, lunch, seats in the West Stand for the match, and an opportunity to meet some of the players (as well as Gazza) after the match.

Five runners-up will each receive a copy of the brand new video game GAZZA'S SUPER SOCCER.

RULES

This competition is open to people aged 16 years and under and completed forms should be received no later than January 8, 1990. Winners will be notified by post in the subsequent two weeks. The first-prize winner must take up his prize within 2 months of being notified and the two tickets are valid for a League fixture only.

The competition will be judged by the directors of Cockerel Books Ltd and their decision is final.

Fill in the competition coupon below in BLOCK CAPITALS and send to: **Cockerel Books**, 23-25 Maddox Street, London, W1R 9LE.

QUESTIONS

1 Gazza has a couple of china animals in his house - what are they?

____

2 When he first started at Newcastle United Gazza was apprentice to a famous footballer - who, and which team did he play for before Newcastle?

____

3 What was Gazza missing when he scored his first goal for Spurs?

____

4 Gazza has a footballing uncle - which League team did he play for?

____

Tie-breaker: complete the following sentence in not more than 15 words:

I think Gazza's great because ....

____

____

____

____

____

____

____

Name ______________________

Address ______________________

____

Daytime tel no ______________ **Age** __________

Video Game

GAZZA'S SUPER SOCCER

Nowadays, being a soccer star doesn't just mean playing football. Gazza has been getting involved with a few other projects since arriving at Tottenham and one of the most recent of these is a video game - GAZZA'S SUPER SOCCER.

In this brand new football game you select and control your team in League or International matches. It has been designed to give the players maximum control of the ball on the screen - you can try taking free kicks like Gazza, bending it round the wall, or dribbling through the opposition, or getting in a good, hard tackle. Though remember, just like the real thing, the referee is going to be on hand to blow the whistle if you go in a bit late!

You can arrange the game so you play with Gazza ... or, if you're feeling brave, against him. You can manage the team you set up throughout the season, do transfer deals, etc.

"It's not quite the same as running out on the park at White Hart Lane, but it's getting close," says Gazza. "It's a great chance to learn how important tactics are in the game, which is sometimes easy to forget when you're dashing round in the thick of it. I'm still trying to beat myself, but the game's got the better of me so far!"

See if you can do better - send away for your own copy of GAZZA'S SUPER SOCCER using the form. We are offering a special discount of 20% when you use the form in this book. Or try to win one of the games in our competition on page 49

SPECIAL 20% DISCOUNT OFFER

Please send me ___ copy/ies of GAZZA'S SUPER SOCCER in the format/s indicated below:

BLOCK CAPITALS PLEASE.

Tapes:	☐ Spectrum	☐ Commodore 64	☐ Amstrad	Offer price **£7.96** (Normal price £9.95)
Disks:	☐ Spectrum	☐ Commodore 64	☐ Amstrad	Offer price **£11.96** (Normal price £14.95)
	☐ Atari ST	☐ Commodore Amiga	☐ IBM PC/ compatibles	Offer price **£15.96** (Normal price £19.95)

I enclose my cheque in the sum of £ ________ made paybale to Entertainment International (UK) Ltd, or please debit my Access/Visa account by this amount.

CARD NO: ☐☐☐☐☐☐☐☐☐☐☐☐☐☐☐☐ **EXPIRY DATE:** ________

NAME ____________________

ADDRESS ____________________

____________________ **TEL NO:** ________

Return this order form to Gazza's Super Soccer Offer, Entertainment International (UK) Ltd, Unit 4 Stannetts, Laindon North Trade Centre, BASILDON, Essex SS15 6DJ

GAZZA FAX

Gazza scored both Newcastle goals in a 2-0 win against Tottenham at St. James's Park on January 23, 1988.

Gazza's favourite pop stars are Neil Diamond and Elvis Presley.

Gazza became Tottenham's most expensive signing in July 1988 when he moved from Newcastle United for £2 million.

Gazza bought his mum and dad a home in Dunston with the signing-on fee he received from Tottenham.

The only time Gazza concentrated at school was in his PE lesson.

Gazza catapulted from novice into the £2 million class in just three seasons and 92 Newcastle United League games.

Gazza's favourite local is the Excelsior Working Men's Club in his home-town of Dunston.

Gazza has been compared with George Best, Billy Bremner, Johnny Giles and Len Shackleton!

CROSSWORD

Here is another crossword to test your endurance and football prowess!

Across

1 Nickname of Gazza's Spurs team-mate Paul Moran (7)
7 Likes to be seen at all the 'right' places (5)
8 One's intended (7)
9 Arrange (4)
10 Terry Venables's role at Tottenham (4)
12 Possible half-time citrus drink (5)
13 What Gazza can do to a defence (7)
16 Terry Venables might do this in the dressing room at half-time if things are not going well (4)
19 First name of one of Gazza's Tottenham midfield team-mates (5)
21 Mitchell, for instance (6)
22 First name of a Spurs goalkeeper (5)
23 Not in the first team...but still playing (7)

Down

1 Two sit on our bench at each match...until used (4)
2 Paul and Clive are a pair of these (6)
3 Gary Mabbutt was one at his former club (5)
4 Gazza's former Spurs and England team-mate (6)
5 Young Spurs winger making his mark (6)
6 Holder of Tottenham's record for League appearances (8)
11 Positions on right or left in old-fashioned line-up (7)
14 Richard Gough became one after leaving Spurs (6)
15 John is Gazza's ...... (6)
17 Expression of regret (4)
18 Bob's the job for this Spurs 'keeper (5)
20 First name of a Spurs physio (4)

LINE QUIZ

Using two straight lines, divide the box into 4 sections. In each section the numbers must total 30.

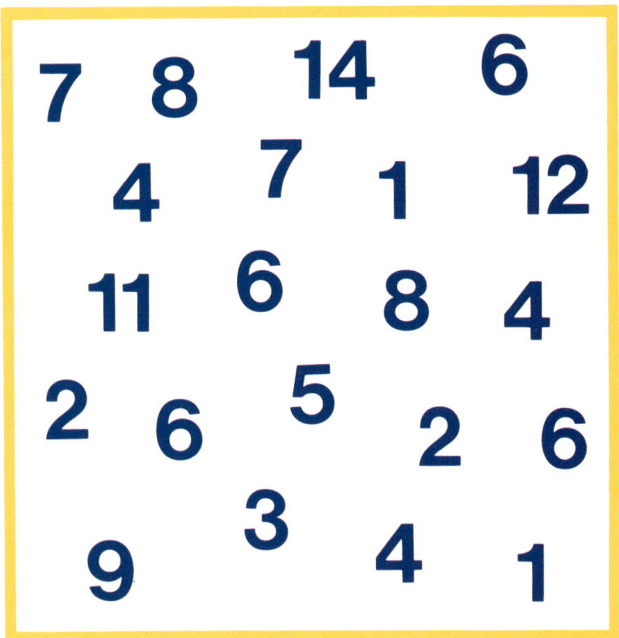

WORD-FIT

Fill in the missing middle word which, when added on to the end of the first word forms a new word and, when placed in front of the second word, forms another word.

1. BIG....BALL
2. MILL....PAPER
3. MARS...ROW
4. OFF....BOARD
5. GOAL....MAN
6. CAN...AIRES
7. WILD....HAM
8. CLAY......PIE

Ball Logic

Study the sequence of numbers, then work out logically the next number.

3

TRI-COUNT

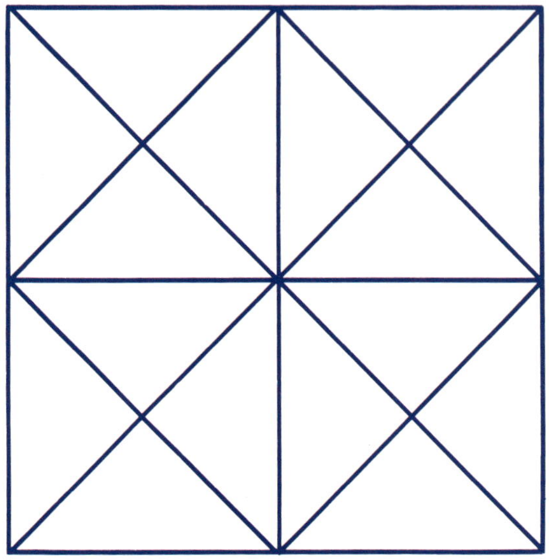

How many triangles are there in this figure?

Ball Logic

Study the sequence of numbers, then work out logically the next number.

2

CLAY COUNT UP

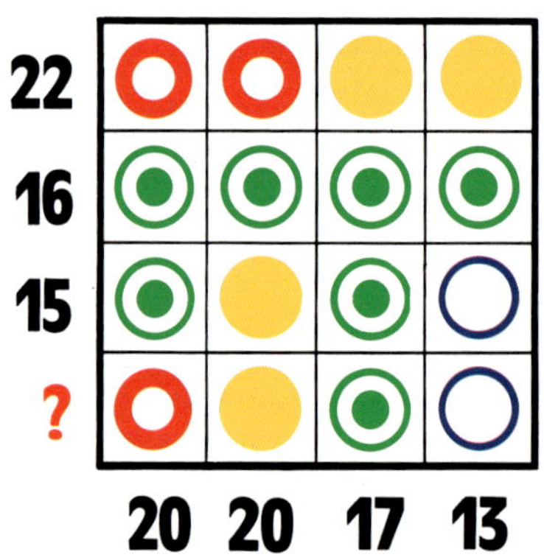

The four different clay pigeons each have a different value. Added together they give the totals at the end of each row and column. What is the total for the bottom row?

Answers on pages 60-61.

Footballers of the Past

Can you identify the footballers of the past in the photographs below?

1 Two forwards who played for Spurs before Gazza was born: can you identify them?

2 Who is this former Liverpool stalwart, now a manager?

3 Gazza has been compared with one of these players - who are they and which team did they play for?

4 Can you recognise this striker, gasping as his shot is saved? He's still to be seen on TV talking about the game with one of the other players featured in this section.

GAZZA FAX

Gazza once won £2,000 on Newcastle's club lottery.

Answers on pages 60-61.

Looking Ahead To The WORLD CUP

It is hard to imagine Paul Gascoigne ever moving abroad to join the Euro exodus, because his interest in football barely leaves these shores.

So when you ask him who is going to win the 1990 World Cup, it is more than patriotism that makes him answer 'England'. Quite simply, he believes that this country plays the best football in the world.

Why then, has England only won the World Cup once?

"It doesn't make sense to me," says Gazza. "We've certainly got the players so it's up to us to get it together and get behind each other. An English side playing with passion and belief is unbeatable.

"I would love to see England win the next World Cup. And I would love to be part of that victory. At the moment we have the players who want to do well and are capable of fulfilling that promise. I honestly feel that 1990 could be our year for the World Cup."

It is a sad fact of our European exile that a player as talented as Gazza has never played in Euro competition at club level. Yet, there is no doubt, that he is as good as any other 21-year-old on the Continent and he is fiercely proud of being English.

"I watch a good deal of Continental football on television and I'm not impressed. Some of it is diabolical - a waste of time. It is clear that they possess good players but they are not always willing to apply themselves.

"I don't really take too much interest in what is happening overseas. Let them worry about us. But if you are asking me who else could win the World Cup then I would have to say the regulars like Brazil, West Germany and Argentina, because of what they have proved in the past.

"Obviously such major soccer powers must have a chance but they would be wrong to underestimate us. I want to be involved in the World Cup, be a regular part of manager Bobby Robson's plans, and it is up to myself to do it.

"I know that if I lined up in a side that featured the likes of Bryan Robson, Peter Shilton, Peter Beardsley and Chris Waddle I would have no reason to feel overawed. Those lads are as good as anybody on this planet and I get annoyed when people keep saying that the average Continental player has more to offer.

"That world stage appeals to me and Chris Waddle would be in his element. He's got as much skill as any Continental player and I know that if we get there he'll prove it.

"They may appear to have better technique and there is no doubt that they pass well. But they also have more time in which to operate and possess many negative aspects in their play which are conveniently ignored by the so-called experts. I'd like to see them producing a bicycle kick with Vinny Jones coming in for the kill!

"Maybe some of them are very skilful and perhaps we miss out a bit in that department. But when things are going against them they tend to give in easily whereas your typical English player will grit his teeth and battle back in the face of adversity.

"The difference is heart - and we've got that in abundance."

GAZZA FAX

When he met 'Loads-a-money' comedian, Harry Enfield, Gazza suggested: "He's not as funny as me!"

Who To Watch in 1990

Division 1 '89-'90

1. **TOTTENHAM HOTSPUR**
2. **Liverpool**
3. **Arsenal**
4. **Manchester United**

Spurs for the Championship! That is the conviction of Paul Gascoigne as he looks forward to the 1989-90 season.

"The Big Four next year are going to be *Spurs, Liverpool, Arsenal* and *Manchester United* - if the Old Trafford lads buck their ideas up," says Gazza.

And the player set to shine next season? Gazza's a home banker on that one too. It's got to be his Spurs team-mate, *David Howells*.

"David's one player that I admired last season," explains Gazza. "He's a young lad who works hard and he's impressed me by the way he's adapted to his first real run in the top flight.

"He could have scored - and he knows this himself - at least three or four times in some games. Because he hasn't done so he has not received the tributes he deserved.

"In fact, people go away saying that he hasn't done well because he's missed chances. They seem to believe that had those opportunities fallen to others they would have put them away.

"But I've told him not to worry about that because at least he's getting in the position to miss them. Who else in the team that day missed three? Nobody, because they weren't in the right place.

"David Howells is going to do well next year. Once he starts scoring he'll be away. So remember - Gazza told you first!"

Two other Spurs youngsters to watch, says Paul, are *Vinny Samways*, already gaining a good deal of first-team experience at White Hart Lane, and flying winger, *Mark Robson*, who only made his debut last term.

"Vinny's learning all the time and I'm convinced that he will have a good season. I'm also impressed by Mark. I know he's a bit thin but if he works on his physique, he'll do OK.

"I want everybody at Tottenham to do well because they're my family now. It's my club, a part of me, in fact my life at the moment.

"What we must do is get a good start and keep it going. I've absolutely loved my first year at Tottenham and I know that we have the makings of a great side.

GAZZA FAX

Before England's 5-0 World Cup qualifier defeat of Albania, manager Bobby Robson described his talented young player as being "daft as a brush". At training next day, Gazza turned up with a brush stuck down his stocking!

hummel
HOLSTEN

"This side is a real football club. We've got a Chairman who wants to do well for the club and who doesn't think about himself. he is prepared to let the manager spend money and has a fantastic manager with unlimited ideas in *Terry Venables*.

"If a player respects his club then he will work hard and give blood and guts for that club. That's what I'm prepared to do for Tottenham.

"It's great to have such a massive club behind you everyone helping each other and wanting to do the business. Tottenham has exactly that."

Meanwhile, in his ambitions for the next season, Gazza cannot help but spare a thought for his former club, *Newcastle United*, who have nosedived into the Second Division.

"I was very upset to see them go down - I still can't believe it. There will be a lot of sad people up there absolutely devastated by relegation.

"But the one thing that can lift you out of the Second Division is spirit - and they've got that up there. I'm keeping my fingers crossed for them."

GAZZA FAX

Gazza used to break-in boots for the great Kevin Keegan and once lost one he was showing to his friends while travelling home on the Newcastle Metro. He asked his dad to explain what had happened to Kevin,and the former England striker said he "hadn't liked the boots anyway."

PUZZLE PAGE ANSWERS

Page 14

Gazza-Word

Across

8. Greats, 9. Tea, 10. Rout, 12. Do, 13. Kit, 14. Imp, 15. Bryan (Robson), 16, Yes, 18. If, 20. One, 22. At, 23. Errors, 26. R.S. (Ray Stewart), 27. No, 28. L.O. (Lawrence Olivier), 29. Swoon, 32. Arsenal, 33. Ger, 35. Lem (Ray Clemence), 37. Hummel, 40. Stiles, 42. Lap, 44. Nape, 46. Eve, 47. West, 48. Mo, 49. Curry, 50. Err, 51. Nay (Nayim).

Down

1. Erik, 2. Party, 3. Assista, 4. Stephen, 5. Bamber, 6. Prayer, 7. Gudni, 11. To, 17. Earn, 19. Fool, 21. Newcastle, 24. Roar, 25. Oss (Ossie), 28. Lane, 30. O.T.T., 31. Age, 34. Emblem, 36. Lesser, 37. Hope, 38. Moncur, 39. Lie, 41. Late, 43. Avon, 45. Park, 47. We.

Page 15

Position Match-up

1. Chris Woods, Rangers
2. Guy Butters
3. Pat Van Den Hauwe, Everton
4. Kevin Ratcliffe, Everton
5. Ronnie Whelan, Liverpool
6. Steve Hodge, Nottingham Forest
7. Bryan Robson, Manchester United
8. Paul Gascoigne, Tottenham Hotspur
9. Chris Waddle
10. Paul Merson, Arsenal
11. Danny Wallace

Letter-fit

1. Ian Rush
2. Gary Lineker
3. Glenn Hoddle
4. Clive Allen
5. Bruce Grobbelaar
6. Chris Waddle
7. Kenny Dalglish
8. Graeme Sharp
9. Peter Beardsley

Page 16

The Great Gazza Football Quiz

1. Northumberland Park
2. Lucien Laurent (France 1930)
3. Santos F.C.
4. Italy
5. Liverpool v. Everton (3-2)
6. Bryan Robson
7. Huracan
8. Ian Botham
9. Fifty-nine caps
10. Morocco
11. Arsenal v. Tottenham (3-2)
12. Albania v. England (0-5)
13. Four times
14. Gary Lineker, he scored six goals
15. Italy and Brazil
16.

a. Rangers
b. Arsenal
c. Everton
d. Liverpool
e. Millwall
f. Manchester United
g. Luton Town
h. Chelsea

Page 17

Face Match

The four players are Paul Stewart, John Polston, Gary Stevens and Erik Thorsveldt.

Ball Logic 1

7 11 13 17 **19**

Page 28

Gazza The Hot Shot

6 + 1 + 10 + 4 = 21
2 + 8 + 5 + 6 = 21
4 + 5 + 10 + 2 = 21
6 + 5 + 10 = 21
10 + 8 + 1 + 2 = 21
6 + 8 + 4 + 2 + 1 = 21

Gascoigne?

Acne, Aeon, Agog, Age, As, Cage(s), Cog(s), Coin(s), Coinage, Cone(s), Egg(s), Gains(s),Gas(es), Gen, Gin(s), Gone, Gong(s), Nose(s), Sag(s), Sage, Sang, Scone(s), Sea(s), Sign(s), Song(s), Son(s).

Guess The Fish?

1. Carp
2. Shark
3. Trout
4. Bass
5. Whale
6. Tuna
7. Haddock
8. Goldfish
9. Sole
10. Seahorse

Page 29

Clay Pigeon Shoot

Gazza will shoot a Large Green Clay next.
The sequence being:
Red Big Blue Small Blue Big Green Small Red Small Green Big Green Big

Play it Again Gazza

The first key played was 4L

Page 40

Spot The Difference

Changes are in the second picture

1. Goalkeeper's shirt is black
2. Gioalkeeper's socks are odd
3. Flask has an extra stripe
4. There is an extra stripe on the mug
5. Missing stripe on right boot
6. Foulup Utd is spelt Foulup Otd
7. Stripes and triangle missing on goalkeeper's shorts
8. Sandwich box lid is black
9. There is no handle on the flask
10. First supporter's jumper is different
11. First supporter's trouser's are black
12. Third supporter has black shoes
13. Third supporter has stripey trousers

14. Footballer's number one has an outline around it
15. Footballer's boot has an extra stripe

World Cup

Low, Cow, Row, Curl, Plod, Clod, Pod, Cod, Up, Do, Loud, Cloud, Lord, Word, Cord, Dour, Pour, Noise.

Page 41

Team Search

A	I	H	B	G	O	C	L	T	D	Y	O	E	Y	T	C	C	F
C	U	S	N	O	R	W	I	C	H	C	I	T	Y	B	A	H	Y
I	M	E	V	E	R	T	O	N	C	H	N	O	T	R	R	A	R
T	S	A	L	U	T	O	N	T	O	W	N	A	D	I	D	R	I
M	O	V	N	L	I	V	C	I	U	E	T	E	Y	S	I	L	I
T	U	T	L	C	H	E	L	S	E	A	T	L	E	T	F	T	Y
P	T	A	T	C	H	U	E	Y	T	I	C	N	M	O	F	O	N
D	H	R	R	E	S	E	T	E	N	V	D	N	A	L	C	N	O
E	A	S	O	L	N	O	S	U	Y	E	D	L	F	R	I	A	C
R	M	E	T	T	Y	H	M	T	W	E	L	I	O	O	T	T	T
B	P	N	H	I	C	A	A	D	E	I	L	V	R	V	Y	H	I
Y	T	A	C	C	H	M	L	M	V	R	M	E	E	E	O	L	Y
C	O	L	A	T	H	E	E	N	H	C	U	B	S	R	F	E	O
O	N	L	S	I	I	N	O	D	S	O	A	N	L	S	Y	T	U
U	T	E	T	F	I	T	E	O	L	O	T	U	I	E	T	I	C
N	W	I	F	O	S	H	A	M	C	O	U	S	N	T	D	C	P
T	P	E	L	A	M	I	L	L	W	A	L	L	P	Y	E	O	T
Y	H	L	I	V	E	R	P	O	O	L	W	E	S	U	T	D	N
S	A	E	V	L	E	E	D	S	U	N	I	T	E	D	R	L	Y

Manchester United

Sheffield Wednesday

West Ham United

Southampton

Liverpool

Charlton Athletic

Tottenham Hotspur

Derby County

Millwall

Aston Villa

Arsenal

Wimbledon

Page 48

Spot The Ball

That's Logic

6 9 13 16 20 **23**
11 13 17 25 32 **37**
20 22 26 34 41 **46**

Page 51

Crossword

Across
1. Sparrow, 7. Poser, 8. Beloved, 9. Sort, 10. Boss, 12. Lemon, 13. Terrify, 16. Rant, 19. Vinny, 21. Thomas, 22. Peter(Guthrie), 23. Reserve.

Down
1. Subs, 2. Allens, 3. Rover, 4. Waddle, 5. Robson, 6. Perryman, 11. Outsides, 14. Ranger, 15. Father, 17. Alas, 18. Mimms, 20. Dave(Butler).

Page 52

Line Quiz

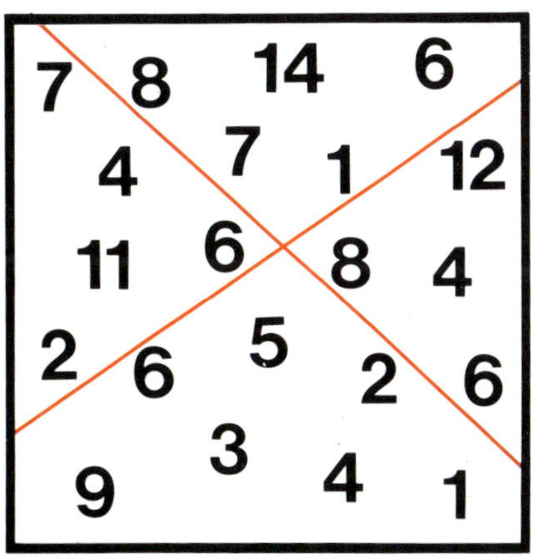

Word Fit

1. BIG**FOOT**BALL
2. MILL**WALL**PAPER
3. MARS**BAR**ROW
4. OFF**SIDE**BOARD
5. GOAL**POST**MAN
6. CAN**CAN**ARIES
7. WILD**WEST**HAM
8. CLAY**PIGEON**PIE

Ball Logic

4 6 9 13 **18**

Tri-Count

There are **28** triangles in the figure

Ball Logic

6 12 15 21 **24**

Clay Count-Up

The missing row = 17
Because:

= 6 = 5
= 4 = 2

Page 53

Footballers Of The Past

1. (Left) Jimmy Greaves and (Right) Alan Gilzean.
2. John Toshack.
3. (Left) Pat Crerand and (Right) George Best, they played for Manchester United.
4. Ian St. John, who of course links up with Jimmy Greaves on Saint and Greavsie.

OLSTEN
THFC
hummel

Welcome

...to the Complete Guide to Android

When Google first revealed Android, there was a wave of excitement throughout the industry. Here was the world's smartest web company making a smartphone. Google's point has always been that there's a space in the fast-developing smartphone market for a brand-new open platform, one that isn't afraid to show its workings and allow developers under the hood. This open-source approach has played very nicely indeed for Google, with Android fast become the darling of the smartphone world.

Android phones have plenty of interesting features to offer, from Flash video and high-quality built-in cameras to high-speed web browsing, GPS navigation and great music playback. Android apps can be quickly tailored to take advantage of the solid hardware on which Android phones are based. The mobile phone has come a long way since the 1980s.

Of course, Android phones are much more powerful than your regular mobile phone, which is why we've put together this guide to the multitude of features even an 'average' Android handset offers. We cover every aspect of setting up and getting the most out of your Android phone, with walkthroughs and tricks outlining the ways to get even more from your device. And with Honeycomb – the first tablet-specific version of Android – now available, we also look at what you can do with a larger screen.

Throughout 2009 and 2010, there was a sort of pioneering spirit surrounding Android. App development outstripped even that for the iPhone, and Android became the fast-growing smartphone sector. It shows no sign of slowing. One thing's for sure, Android is here to stay.

This is our guide to the best that Android represents. We'd also love to hear which apps you admire, and what you think of this guide.

Rosemary Hattersley
Editor

Editor
Rosemary Hattersley
rosemary_hattersley@idg.co.uk

Production editors
Rob Woodcock, Jon Lysons

Writers
Rob Clymo, Ross Catanzariti, Spencer Dalziel, Matt Egan, Andrew Harrison, Rosemary Hattersley, Ginny Mies, Melissa Perenson, Carrie-Ann Skinner, Sandra Vogel

Art editors
Dominik Tomaszewski
Bob Cree

Production & Marketing

Production manager
Richard Bailey
richard_bailey@idg.co.uk

Assistant marketing manager
Emma van Beurden
emma_vanbeurden@idg.co.uk

Publishing

Editor
Matt Egan
matt_egan@idg.co.uk

Editor in chief
Mark Hattersley
mark_hattersley@idg.co.uk

Publisher
Simon Jary
simon_jary@idg.co.uk

Publisher
Mustafa Mustafa
mustafa_mustafa@idg.co.uk

Managing director
Kit Gould

The Complete Guide to Android is a published by IDG Communications, the world's leading IT media, research and exposition company. With more than 300 publications in 85 countries, read by more than 100 million people each month, IDG is the world's leading publisher of computer magazines and newspapers.
IDG Communications, 101 Euston Road, London NW1 2RA.

Project management and print by Fusion Media - tel: 03309 991 240, email info@fusionmedialtd.co.uk

Contents

Index

Introducing Android

Chapter 1